A moustache,
poison and
blue glasses!

BROMLEY

TALES OF THE TOUR DE FRANCE

A moustache,
poison and
blue glasses!

BROMLEY

This English Language Edition is published by
Bromley Books
11 The Terrace, Barnes, London SW13 0NP
Tel: +44 (0)20 8876 4671   Fax: +44 (0)20 8878 3858

Bromley Books is a division of Bromley Television International Ltd
© Bromley Books, 1999

Original Danish version: 'Stars & Winecarriers'
© Svend Novrup & P.Haase & Sons, Forlag, 1996

A catalogue record of this book is available from the British Library.
ISBN 0-9531729-1-0

Designed by Ammonite Design Associates
Printed and bound in the UK by Polestar
Photography:
Photosport International, on pages 3, 39, 51, 63, 151,
157, 163, 171, 184, 185
Graham Watson, on page 181
Roger St Pierre, on pages 14, 15, 27, 33, 81, 99
Presse Sports, on pages 9, 23, 43, 57, 61, 71, 74, 85, 93,
103, 107, 113, 123, 125, 131, 135
Pol-foto, on pages 119, 143, 155

Contents

Acknowledgements

I first met the author, Svend Novrup when he came to London... for of all things, the World Bridge Championships. He called me and suggested a meeting at the White House hotel where the Championships were taking place. 'But I am not Omar Sharif, I don't play bridge' I told him, 'I am into sport, cycling, you know the big outdoors.'

'But so I am' he said, 'Have you not heard me commentate on cycling for Eurosport.' 'No' I said, 'I listen to David Duffield.' 'Ah, that is because you do not speak Danish!' came his reply.

And so that was how I first met Svend Novrup, this crazy Danish journalist with a mad passion for cycling and the history of the Tour de France. This English edition is the result of that meeting.

Special thanks must go to: Anne-Marie, who translated the original manuscript, Nina Jensen at P. Haase & Sons – the original publishers, Luke Evans at CycleSport, Martin Ayres, David Duffield, Roger St. Pierre, Graham Watson, and John Pierce at Miroir Archive-Photosport International for permission to reproduce the photos, and finally a sincere thanks to Les Woodland, the editor, for his work and many helpful suggestions.

David Bromley

Foreword

You are in Paris at the turn of the century, enjoying the sights of the French capital, when you see 60 strangely dressed men cycling up a street. They are on a journey, you are told, that will take them around France for three weeks... that over 1,500 miles will be tackled in six stages, and that they face an average of over 253 miles per day...

...they face terribly rough roads, strewn in places with stones and potholes... with clouds of thick dust on sunny days and then muddy ruts when it rains...

...they start late at night, or before the break of dawn, to ride anything between 15 and 22 hours on single speed bicycles with laid back angles, long wheel bases and tyres that were prone to puncture.

These were the conditions facing those sixty riders or perhaps pioneers would be a better word, that started the very first Tour de France... and let us not forget that until one week before hand, the race was going to be over five weeks, not three!

The journalists covering this epic event did not have access to today's race radio and TV monitors. Travelling as best they could, sometimes by motorised vehicle, but more often by train and bicycle, their job was to report the events of the day as best they could. They wrote of heroic deeds by these hardy men on bicycles, the 'Giants of the Road', in prose that enthralled the French public, but also of the intrigue and sabotage that went with the early Tours as the riders often faced hostile partisan crowds.

Over the years, the roads, bicycles, and communications have changed beyond recognition. But the tenacity and courage of the riders has remained constant.

Today's Tour de France is conducted in the full glare of the spotlight of the world's media. There are TV cameras on motorbikes and in helicopters, plus radio reporters, photographers and some 1,000 journalists to record every aspect of the greatest free sporting spectacle in the world.

But for the riders the Tour remains the same. To compete, to win..., even to finish the Tour de France, that is a great achievement in itself. In 1955 I rode to Paris to see the first two British riders ever to complete the 'Grand Boucle'. Tony Hoare was the last man overall, the 'Lanterne Rouge', the Red Lamp, as it's known. He and the other survivor, Brian Robinson, received heroes' welcomes for their performances. Indeed, Brian Robinson's achievements have gone down in history and form part of my Eurosport colleague, Svend Novrup's delightful book of fascinating tales of the Tour de France.

Svend is passionate about the cycling and in particular, the Tour de France and has with great dedication, sifted through these and many, many other stories to produce this book, to give an insight into the courage of the riders, the problems they faced and their ambitions to finish the Tour.

Some have failed to finish, like my good friend Tom Simpson, who died so tragically on the barren volcanic mountain of Mont Ventoux, or more recently the terrible accident which took the life of the Olympic Champion, Fabio Casartelli on the descent of the col du Portet d'Aspect.

So when you read this book, and you relive the heroic deeds, spare a thought for all those riders, who since 1903, have through their tenacity and ambition, their courage and sweat, contributed to making the Tour de France, what it is, simply the greatest bike race in the World.

David Duffield
Cycling Commentator, Eurosport.

Introduction
The road to the Tour

The inspiration: Henri Desgrange had an impressive cycling background; a world record 100km tricycle 2 hours, 41 minutes and 58 seconds in 1895, while two years earlier had become the first man to establish world record figures for the unpaced 'hour' covering 21 miles, 1674 yards.

Introduction – The road to the Tour

Rik Van Looy rides like a cat. He's crouched and tense and ready to spring. But cats usually chase mice. This time the mice are chasing the cat. They're strung on his wheel, praying the misery will end. And then, after a fashion, it does.

Van Looy wears unusually brief black shorts. They show the cord muscles rolling in his thighs. Suddenly they twang tighter. It's the only warning and the mice miss it.

The Emperor of Herentals, world champion and king of the classics, rides off the front with a kilometre to go. His back curves, his melon mouth grimaces, and his beaky nose points down at his tyre, up at the road, back down at the tyre.

The mice scramble, fighting now, scrabbling over themselves to reach him. A radio commentator fights to hold his microphone, his sanity and his bladder as he screams how the Belgian has raged past a crossing, cleared the shadow beneath a bridge and is even now just 500 metres from the line. And the chase can't make a whisker's length progress on him.

Fists pound dingy tables in a million cafés across Europe. Faces tighten, eyes turn off as the brain takes in only the words from the radio. And then Van Looy wins. Muscles loosen. Van Looy vanishes into the crowd. Drinks are sought, backs slapped, and work begins on rehashing yet another day at the Tour de France.

The Tour de France... It's the drama of the sport that catches you first. The great riders and their never-ending struggle with each other. The *domestiques*, the humble team riders normally so vital and anonymous but suddenly thrown into the spotlight. These are the incidents that prove, time and again, that reality exceeds even fantasy in the Tour de France.

And then it's the theatricality. The team managers who set the strategies and zigzag through the field as they hang from their windows to talk to the riders, to reporters.

And what of the practical things? How do you feed and accommodate several thousand people at new places every night? How do you organise the stream of news? How do you share the sun, the moon and the wind between television, radio and newspapers?

Who was this man Christophe who had to repair his own bike three times? Why didn't he just get a new one?

What is the strange story of the Italian who won the Tour only to be found murdered by the roadside?

Is it really possible that an Algerian drank wine, slept for two hours and then set off in the wrong direction... and grew rich on the story?

And how about the riders who've won five times: did Indurain have it tougher than Anquetil or Merckx? And why did the fabled Fausto Coppi win it only twice?

For that matter, what was the Tour like in 1903 when the roads were filthy tracks, the bike barely invented and gears and freewheels still a dream?

Like you, I wanted to know. This is the result of a huge amount of enthusiasm and curiosity. It's not a reference book, although I have added some 'not so hard and cold facts' of the Tour's story over the years, along with the winners of the three main jerseys. Nor is it a book of results, of sporting achievements in the last 20 years, because so many other books that have done that.

No, this is a picture of the Tour, its history and its unique spirit. I've chosen the characters for their personality, not for their abilities. I don't even look just at the winners. The only place you'll find them all is the index at the back. Often I've turned the spotlight on riders who've had only supporting roles but whose exploits make a good story.

Sometimes the 'facts' are tangled. For instance, I read once of Henri Desgrange raising the flag for the first Tour de France to ride off into the misty dawn. Well, it's romantic but in fact the Tour started at 3.16pm. And Georges Abran was the starter, not Desgrange.

It doesn't get any better with questions like 'Why is the leader's jersey yellow?' Some say it's because it matched the yellow paper of Desgrange's paper, *L'Auto*. Well, maybe. But the Tour itself says clothing was in short supply at the time and that yellow jerseys – an unpopular colour – were the only ones he could get. Not that he minded – they served a double purpose.

I've dramatised some of the stories, not necessarily in the actual words because they've been lost, but in ways that are based on fact. I hope they'll help you enjoy the story even more and that like me you will delight in the history of the Tour de France – that mixture of sport, politics, entertainment, economy and publicity that make it what it is, not just in France but across the world.

Svend Novrup

Le Numéro : 1 Centime

ADMINISTRATION
PUBLICITÉ
Rue du Faubourg Montmartre, 10
PARIS (9e Arr¹)

TÉLÉPHONE : 227-99
ADMINISTRATION 233-13

Adresse Télégraphique : Vélauto-Paris

Directeur-Rédacteur en Chef :
HENRI DESGRANGE

ABONNEMENTS :
Un mois Un an
LES DÉPARTEMENTS. 10 fr 20 fr
ÉTRANGER 15 fr 28 fr

L'abonnement sera fait chaque jour au
Bureau du journal.

L'Auto

AUTOMOBILE — CYCLISME

ATHLÉTISME, YACHTING, AÉROSTATION, ESCRIME, POIDS et HALTÈRES, HIPPISME, GYMNASTIQUE, ALPINISME

LE TOUR DE FRANCE — LE DÉP

Organisé par L'AUTO du 1er au 19 Juillet 1903

A SEMENCE

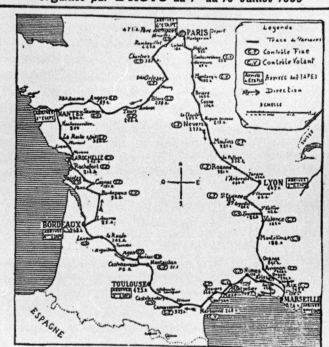

L'ITINÉRAIRE DU TOUR DE FRANCE

AUCOUTURIER

JOS. FISCHER

M. GARIN

1

Fiasco, scandal... and success

Henri Desgrange: the formidable Editor of *L'Auto* and "the Father of the Tour".
Far left: The front cover of *L'Auto* with the first Tour route. Paris-Lyon-Marseille-Toulouse-Bordeaux-Nantes-Paris – 1,510 miles.

Fiasco, scandal... and success

'Patron, I have an idea.' November 1902 was grey and rainy and things weren't going well at *L'Auto*. Desgrange had set out to sink his rival but he wasn't a man for ideas. When Pierre Giffard at *Le Vélo* ran a race from Bordeaux to Paris, Desgrange promoted another. Readers were delighted at the choice but it was no reason to start buying *L'Auto*. And so it went on.

Now Desgrange's backers were asking pointed questions about their money. The time had come for a crisis meeting. There were perhaps half a dozen of them there, including a young cycling and rugby reporter called Géo Lefèvre, who'd been poached from *Le Vélo* for his brightness. Now, in the gloom of the paper's boardroom at 10 rue Faubourg Montmartre, close to the Folies Bergères, he came up with his idea.

'Why don't we organise a race bigger than anyone has ever seen?' he asked. 'Like the six-day races on the track but going from town to town.'

Desgrange hesitated.

'If I understand you, you're talking about a Tour de France?' The word *tour* in French is closer to 'circuit' than its English concept of a promenade. Lefèvre watched his expression carefully.

Desgrange wasn't bursting with enthusiasm. The world was, though. It was a time of optimism and excitement and progress. There hadn't been a war since 1871 and folk said there'd never be another. Cures were being found for deadly diseases. It looked like men could fly. And people throughout the world were discovering their bodies, looking after them, giving themselves new challenges through sport. The harder the better.

Desgrange knew about challenges. He'd set the world's first hour record on May 11, 1893, by riding 35.325km on the Buffalo track at Neuilly. He added record after record for another two years, among them the 100km on a bicycle and on a trike. Bike racing had been a wow at the rebirth of the Olympic Games in 1896 and 1900. Six-day races had moved from roller-skates to bicycles, even though there was as yet nothing better than a single fixed gear.

But Desgrange wasn't at all sure of Lefèvre's idea. He hesitated, looked at his watch and announced it time for lunch. He and Lefèvre walked to the Taverne Zimmer in the Boulevard Montmartre. The subject wasn't mentioned until coffee. Then Lefèvre ran through it again.

The race would go from town to town, welcomed for the publicity and the honour of its company. The riders would start together each day but with the time difference they had at the finishing line on the day before.

Desgrange would say no more than it was 'interesting.' He'd mention it to Victor Goddet, *L'Auto*'s financial director, to test his reaction. And to Desgrange's surprise he agreed.

Fifty riders were the least that Desgrange would accept. Too many would give up – or their bikes would – during six stages covering 2,428km and the race would flop if too few made it to Paris. On May 20, 1903, he announced it would cost 10 francs to enter, the organisers would book hotels but riders had to arrange their own meals.

Only 27 had entered by May 30. Six days later Desgrange pleaded: 'Participants in the Tour de France can be sure that they will not spend more money during the race than if they stayed at home in Paris. The hoteliers will offer inexpensive meals because it is an honour and good advertising to be host to our participants. And everyone should remember that for 10 francs he is in competition for a first prize of 3,000 francs.

'You only get one such opportunity.'

It helped. Entrant number 50 signed on 48 hours before the deadline of June 15. Another 28 managed to enter later, which led the Tour to allow just the first 60 to turn up at the Café Réveil-Matin in Montgeron, south of Paris, on July 1, 1903.

Georges Abran stroked his enormous moustache and stepped forward to drop the flag. Several hundred spectators were there to see him. There were musicians and drink-sellers. Desgrange, still doubtful about his race, decided to stay away as much as he could.

The rue Jean Jaurès past the café – still there and looking much as it did nine decades ago – was dusty hard gravel. Tall slender trees make it a traditional French avenue. The bar was a regular venue for local cyclists attracted by its reputation for steak and fries and many of the region's races started there. Desgrange knew the family that owned it.

The riders changed in the cafe cellar and emerged to collect their heavy, clumsy bikes from the walls outside. They had hats and caps of different shapes and sizes against the sun. And at 3.16pm the flag dropped and they set off gently for the first day of the Tour de France.

They were in no hurry. They wouldn't finish until Lyon – 467km away. The following day.

Lefèvre showed more speed. His job was to ride with the race as referee, then get to the furthest station that would get him to the finish before the riders. It was fortunate that he was champion of his club. Desgrange expected a lot of his 26-year-old. Not only would he control the race but he'd send back dispatches as well, which Desgrange and more particularly Olivier Margot would turn into vainglorious epics. They set the style that became L'Auto's throughout its life and then, after its doors were nailed shut for collaborating with the Nazis, that of its successor, L'Equipe.

Of one race, Desgrange wrote: 'There are four of them. Their legs, like giant levers, will power onwards for sixty hours; their muscles will grind up the kilometres; their broad chests will heave with the effort of the struggle; their hands will clench on to their handlebars; with their eyes they will observe each other ferociously; their backs will bend forward in unison for barbaric breakaways; their stomachs will fight against hunger, their brains against sleep. And at night a peasant waiting for them by a deserted road will see four demons passing by, and the noise of their desperate panting will freeze his heart and fill it with terror.'

On July 3, though, they left Lefèvre's words much as he wrote them.

'To experience the decisive part of the stage, I have taken my place alongside the impressive highway which – framed by trees whose crowns come together in darkness – leads from Nevers to Moulin. I am sitting in the ditch with my bike between my legs, waiting for the leaders. Time seems endless, but finally around 1am two figures appear.

'I rush forward and yell: 'Who are you?'

'Garin' yells one of them with a cheerful voice.

'Pagie' says the other, and before they disappear round the next bend I hear loud laughter and an exclamation on the lines of 'Surely it must be past your bedtime, young man!"

The riders impressed Lefèvre. He ended with the words: 'The Tour de France requires real men. Wimps should stay at home!'

Géo Lefèvre didn't make it to Lyon before Maurice Garin. It didn't stop him judging the winner, though. Gaps between riders were enormous. There were only six stages but the 21st and final finisher in Paris was 64 hours 47 minutes and 22 seconds behind Garin. Even the runner-up was 2 hours 49 minutes behind.

Garin's greatest rival should have been Hippolyte Aucouturier, who'd won Bordeaux-Paris and Paris-Roubaix that year. But Aucouturier often had stomach trouble – from drinking too much water, it was said – and a bug had struck him again. He didn't finish the first stage but he did win two more, since the rules allowed riders to rejoin the race on condition they were out of the running for the overall prizes.

As with track six-days, where riders really did compete every hour of the day, the Tour rode day and night. Stages started at different times to cope with the distance: Lyon at 2.30am, Marseille 10.30pm, Toulouse 5am, Bordeaux 11pm, and Nantes at 9pm. All but the first began in darkness. Tactics were banned and riders had to make their own repairs. Other races allowed pacing by cars or helpers, but not the Tour.

It was hardly surprising, then, that there were as many as three rest days between stages.

The hardship and bravery gripped France. Reports in *L'Auto* say between 1,000 and 2,000 cyclists were waiting to escort Garin to the finish at the Parc des Princes track in Paris. It was a triumph, even allowing for any exaggeration.

L'Auto had a special edition on the streets within seven minutes – an astonishing achievement even now. They sold instantly. *L'Auto* printed 14,178,474 papers in the whole year of 1903. And eventually it put *Le Vélo* out of business.

But Desgrange wasn't satisfied. France's other papers hadn't followed the race as much as he'd hoped and there were red numbers in the accounts. He doubted there'd be another. But over time his mood changed and he announced race number two.

This time 27 of the 88 entrants finished in Paris. But what a race. Riders were clubbed on mountain passes. There were demonstrations and attacks. Protesters scattered nails in front of rivals, then turned on the police and officials. Lefèvre had to fire shots into the air to calm the riot.

There were tales of riders paced or even towed by cars. One spoke of a car trailing string and a cork, which a competitor clenched between his teeth.

Aucouturier broke his bike on the first day and lost two hours. When he then won four of the remaining five stages, the public were baffled that he wasn't named the overall winner. But then who was?

For months it was Maurice Garin again. But scandal broke on November 30, 1904. The first four had taken a train, it emerged. They would all be disqualified, all of them banned, one for life. French cycling officials delayed the news for fear of a riot, so great was the hysteria surrounding this new race.

The victory was handed to 20-year-old Henri Cornet, to this day still the youngest winner, and the French nicknamed him *Le Rigolo*, or 'The Fake'. He'd been three hours behind Garin.

'The race has been killed by the very emotions it has unleashed,' Desgrange mourned. 'I fear the second race will have been the last.' But it wasn't. He'd pulled a magnificent publicity trick and he knew it. Let's face it – he'd been a publicist at the Clément tyre factory before taking on *L'Auto*. Papers that had overlooked the Tour now waded in with criticism, advice, admonishment and even suggestions.

'Finally on the streets, avenues, in restaurants, people are talking about my race,' Desgrange said. 'They laugh, or they rage, but they are talking. This means that the Tour de France is set on a course of success.' So he ran another.

Again there were problems.

'*Nouveaux actes de sabotage,*' says the Tour history book. '*Des manifestants sement de clous sur le parcour*' – new acts of sabotage; demonstrators scatter nails on the road. It must have sounded like machine-gun fire. Only Peugeot's Louis Trousselier of the 60 starters avoided puncturing, and he went on to win the Tour. Many of the strong riders were 12 hours behind him.

Again Desgrange was aflame. What do these irresponsible elements think they're playing at? Do they not realise they're putting a noble sport and its participants in danger? It was all good copy for the newspaper silly season.

Desgrange had established the Tour de France.

A moustache, poison and blue glasses

2

Pulling their legs

The first double winner: Lucien Petit-Breton, victorious in 1907 and 1908. Originally born Lucien Mazan in Plesse, France in 1883, he grew up in Buenos Aires, Argentina. Because of his tiny size, nicknamed 'Petit-Breton', yet he was one of the great champions and his average speed for the 1907 Tour remained the intact for 24 years.

Pulling their legs

No good idea lasts long. Not even the Tour. The one thing they knew in Montmartre was that it had to be renewed. But how? Again, it wasn't Desgrange who came up with the answer. Not the permanent answer anyway. It was another journalist, Alphonse Steines.

In 1905 the Tour stretched to 11 stages, almost 3,000km, and it went over the Ballon d'Alsace in the Vosges. It experimented, too, with an alp near Grenoble. But mountains were dangerous. Few peasants crossed them on foot and cyclists certainly never did. Indeed there was much debate – a lot of it stimulated by Desgrange – about whether it was humanly possible to cycle up the Ballon anyway. When it did prove possible, Desgrange wrote that 'the courage of men knows no bounds.'

Alphonse Steines, though, wanted something bigger than the Ballon d'Alsace. He suggested the Pyrénées.

'We must have more mountain stages,' he urged. 'We must send the riders on to the highest Alps and we must let them conquer the Pyrénées.'

Desgrange was typically doubtful.

'But what if it fails? What if one of the riders injuries themselves or at worst even dies. People will call me a murderer.' Anyway, he'd made up his mind. He had another plan. 'We can score political points and we can pull their collective German legs at the same time. We'll make the Tour international! We'll send it over the border into those areas which became so shamefully German after the war in 1870-71. For a single day we'll turn Lothringen into Lorraine.'

Steines knew when he was beaten. But he still hankered after the Pyrénées. There'd be other Tours. He could wait. In the meantime the Tour de France could be an international peacemaker, opening frontiers.

The German government had few qualms. War had been abolished, life was optimistic and nationalism wasn't very visible in Elsass-Lothringen. What's more, both Berlin and the governor of Lothringen – the nephew of Count Zeppelin – spotted a little international prestige. Zeppelin saw it as keeping in with the French part of his population, diplomacy which could make his position in Germany stronger than merely the administrator of an area that 'wasn't really German'.

The paperwork was settled. Even the German police agreed not to stop speeding cyclists. Desgrange noted privately that a German policeman would overlook anything if it was an order. In public, he wrote that French policemen could learn a lesson from German tolerance and stop fining cyclists for riding too fast.

Whatever the French police made of it, the Germans were delighted. The governor suggested finishing a stage at Metz the following year. But he could hardly have imagined the consequences. The French-speakers were so delighted that they put up French-language banners for the first time since 1871. They hadn't seen their language in public since they became involuntarily German and their patriotism made a charged atmosphere. The finishing stretch was decked in French flags. And French riders were cheered home with shameless bias.

'*Vive le Tour de France!*'

'*Vive Petit-Breton!*'

'*Vive Trousselier!*'

The finish was dramatic. Emile Georget and Louis Trousselier sprinted side by side, shoulder to shoulder over the line. Nobody knew who had won. Desgrange asked his judges. They weren't sure. Maybe Gorget just had it, maybe not. Desgrange placed them joint first. A double French victory. It couldn't have been better.

Well, it could have been better. For the governor, certainly. The rise in French feeling began to unsettle him as nationalism grew during 1908 and 1909. War was coming. He had to change his mind. For some years the Tour de France would no longer be a messenger of peace.

A moustache, poison and blue glasses

3

The Count and the wine carriers

A different era: the village fountain was a popular stop for even the greatest riders.

The Count and the wine carriers

'*Maître...* the gentlemen Dargassies and Gauban.' Two athletic young men entered the beautiful room of a castle near Toulouse. The gorgeous furniture, perfectly hand-crafted, tastefully complemented the decorations on the walls. They were impressed, but they were also curious. Who was this Count Pépin de Gontaud who had asked their help as cyclists?

He didn't disappoint. He shone with idealism and he was in good shape if one overlooked a bit of a belly. His dress was modern for 1907 and his handlebar moustache was well kept. He addressed his guests in a light tone.

'Gentlemen, as I have hinted in my letter, the reason you are here is bicycle racing. This Tour de France is a magnificent idea that I would like to support. Not only that but I would like to participate, and preferably finish.

'Now, unlike you gentlemen, I haven't had time to race. I have estates to run and attending to them and a large number of staff is very demanding. But as Baron de Coubertin of the Olympic Games put it, the important thing is not to win but to take part.

'I wish to take part, gentlemen! I can not win. I will not even be among the first to cross the finish line. But if you will help me, I will finish the race. It is a personal ambition, of course, but it is also for the good of your fine sport.'

Jean Dargassies and Henri Gauban looked at each other in surprise. They had expected many things but not this. The nobility on bikes, when cyclists were still rowdy and antisocial. Could there be better advertising? On the other hand they had their own ambitions. Now they were being asked to ride for the count and not to finish in front of him. Did they have to make a spectacle of themselves with this aristocrat who wanted to play at bicycle racing?

They were bike riders, not smooth talkers. They struggled to explain. It would cost them a fortune in lost prizes and engagements. And much though it would be wonderful to have a count in the field, it was perhaps not for them to pay the price.

The objections were no surprise.

'I understand perfectly and I don't expect you to do this for free. I am going to buy three bikes of the new, lighter type and each of you will receive one as your property. I will arrange special room and board and even the winner of the race will envy your pay.

'I am offering you, gentlemen, an easy, entertaining and profitable Tour. Please meet me at the start at the Port Bineau in Paris on July 8 at 5.30am. These envelopes contain your first wages.'

The count was not used to contradiction. His charisma quelled his guests' doubts. They no longer searched for words. Together they assured the count he now had the two best helpers he could have wished. They moved to leave the room with a bow, but the count stopped them.

'We must celebrate! We must get to know each other before we have to endure so much together. Come! Let us study all the 4,488 kilometres together. There are more mountains than before. And you must remember to bring your passports with you. We will be riding through both Switzerland and Germany. The Tour is to bring people closer.

'We also have to plan what we are to enjoy on the way. I am completely useless without food and wine.'

He put an arm round his new helpers and led them to the next room and a table laid for three.

'Jacques, ask the kitchen to begin serving... and please pour some wine. We are going to celebrate the happiest trio that ever cycled round France!'

It truly was a celebration, an opulent meal with vintage wines and countless delicacies. Their sport was toasted time and again with raised glasses and soon folk songs praising the wine began to sneak in. A fine cognac came with the coffee and only long after midnight could the servants confirm that the three were snoring in their rooms – and in such a condition that the following day's training would not be the most important of their lives.

Some time next morning the two new employees found their way home, loaded with iron that good red wine had put in their veins.

There was no reason to line up at the head of the field at the Pont Bineau. They didn't even hurry away when the race started.

The drivers of the two official cars, an innovation of 1907, watched, shrugged, gave up on them and drove off with the rest of the field.

The crowd, though, paid more attention. Rumours had spread for weeks of this strange young nobleman – something he'd encouraged himself – and spectators cheered as he passed. He replied by waving his cap and blowing kisses to the prettiest girls.

The little party rode for a few hours on bread and wine. But then the count decided it was time to stop at a cosy inn. They entered, took their time with a lavish evening meal and local wines, then rolled on towards the end of the stage, singing as they went.

They were in no hurry. They took 12 hours and 20 minutes longer than Emile Georget to ride the 398km from Roubaix to Metz and the timekeepers were hopping mad. The Tour hadn't yet decided to eliminate riders who took too long. And, a count being a count and publicity the only reason for the race, it couldn't even make up a new rule on the spot. They just had to wait.

And to everyone's surprise, the party completed four stages.

One day they found a fellow competitor in a ditch, exhausted by trying to stay with the best. There was no broom wagon to collect the fallen. The man had simply been left. Pépin stepped off his bike and got the disillusioned cyclist to his feet with the aid of his helpers.

'We need to get some strength back into you, my good man,' he announced. 'You are going to have to ride a couple more kilometres before we get to an inn, and then a little food and wine will do the trick.' The revived casualty was so grateful that he joined the count as his third helper.

Sadly, even a personal team couldn't get the baron through the race. He brought them to a halt during the fifth stage from Lyon to Grenoble.

'Gentlemen, you have been loyal and made it the experience of a lifetime for me to take part in the Tour de France. From the town at which we shall shortly be arriving, I will take the train back to Toulouse. You are now free of obligation to me and you may finish the race if you so desire.'

The three stood with their employer. They were as far behind as he was and in no condition to continue without his patronage. They arrived at the station together. The count bought his ticket and there were emotional farewells. He took each by the hand and pressed into it a bundle of notes. Each was to count more than the 5,000 francs that the year's winner would receive. The nobleman had been true to his word.

As the three wine-carriers stood on the platform, their leader waved goodbye from the train, out of the Tour de France and out of their lives.

There is a twist to this story. The Tour's rules did not allow tactics. They certainly didn't allow one rider to hire the services of another. Pépin was the first to bring his own paid helpers, something we now consider normal. But it took another four years and a change of social class and certainly of nationality before Desgrange reacted.

But what the count got away with, the French rider Maurice Brocco couldn't. He, like other riders since, was a good all-rounder who realised there was more money in helping others than winning races himself. Which led Desgrange to write in *L'Auto* that 'he is unworthy of participating in our race; he is a *domestique!*'

And that's how the name came to humble team-mates who sacrifice their chances for their star. They are the team's domestics, the menials.

It wasn't a name that Brocco cared for. Upset at what Desgrange had written, he decided to put things straight. He broke away when the race entered the Pyrénées, crossed the Tourmalet and Aubisque alone and finished 21 minutes ahead of Gustave Garrigou, the eventual winner.

And was Desgrange impressed?

The next day he wrote: 'In the Pyrénées, Brocco confirmed that in the previous days he had not run his own race but sold himself to others. He deserves punishment. Immediate disqualification.'

A moustache, poison and blue glasses

4

A walk in the mountains

So tough are the Mountains: In 1959 a helper clears away the snow for Charly Gaul of Luxembourg. The winner of the 1958 Tour, this enigmatic and tormented individual was a major star of the fifties and one of the finest climbers in bad weather that the Tour has seen.

A walk in the mountains

'Well then, write about the Pyrénées! Then you'll see for yourself what people think of them. Total madness! It's far too dangerous. We'll have blood on our hands!'

Henri Desgrange exploded at his desk. Alphonse Steines had never stopped hinting at the mountains and Desgrange was exhausted by the man and his ridiculous ideas. Funny... Steines thought he'd been rather subtle about it.

The father of the Tour – a title he was happy to take from Géo Lefèvre – was enraged. His whole body exuded agitation. But this was familiar territory for Steines, and certainly better than indifference. At least Desgrange was paying attention, and that was important. What's more, he'd said 'Write about the Pyrénées!'

Steines wasn't going to wait for him to change his mind. He sat at his black, upright typewriter and poured out his heart about why 1910 should take on the mountains of the south. He wrote of the towering majesty of the Peyresourde, the Aspin, Tourmalet and Aubisque. He spoke of the challenge for modern riders and equipment, their fitness and their greater competition. He thought it was wonderful.

People were appalled. They came to Desgrange and demanded how he could send men over mountain tracks that were dangerous when clear and blocked by snow for all but a few weeks. It was ridiculous. Foolish. Terrible. And it shouldn't be done.

Desgrange was delighted.

There was now every reason it should be done. They would be a publicity coup, the Pyrénées. The riders would cross the mountains somehow. But Desgrange wanted a triumph, not blood. So he dreamed up the *voiture balai*, the broom wagon, a van to follow the stragglers and pick up the fallen.

But the roads were still goat tracks, the snow unpredictable. If people who knew the mountains said it couldn't – or at least oughtn't – be done, then maybe disaster loomed. Bears waited. So Desgrange sent Steines to find out. Steines had organised the stage in the south for some years, the mountains were his idea, and therefore he could go in his own car and check for himself. Then he'd see.

Doubt first came when Steines read in Pau that a new Mercedes-Benz had crashed as it tried to cross the Tourmalet. He was no more certain when he visited a Monsieur Blanchet, the official responsible for roads in the Pyrénées and one of *L'Auto*'s readers.

'Impossible!' he said, at the same time patronising and amused. 'Especially on the Aubisque, where the roads are either too small or non-existent.'

Steines had come a long way.

'But we can handle that. We have the resources when it's for the Tour. What would it cost to build up the roads across the Aubisque?'

Blanchet thought about 5,000 francs. Steines got through by phone to Paris first time – a miracle then. Desgrange grimaced and offered 3,000. You got a great deal for 3,000 francs in 1910 when an egg cost five centimes. The offer struck Blanchet as a good deal more than he'd had before Steines arrived at his door, and he'd become the man who brought good roads to the region. He'd have a place in history. And he became very enthusiastic.

'Bravo, Steines! Work will begin tomorrow.'

That was the Aubisque. The next day it was the Tourmalet. The locals at the foot shook their heads. Crossing in May was hopeless. In four weeks, perhaps, almost certainly in the middle of July. But even so... They looked at this elegant Parisian in his shirt, leggings and leather city shoes and shook their heads.

'It may be possible,' some of the hardier ones ventured, 'but you'd need to dress rather differently, *monsieur*.'

Steines hired an experienced driver, collected a large snow shovel and a handful of sacks to put under the tyres, and off they set.

The first six kilometres were fine, if a little shaky on narrow, uneven roads that strained the suspension. The axles received frequent heavy thumps. And then the going got really tough. The engine coughed, the tyres span on the snow and running water... and then the car stuck in a drift. Steines climbed out with his shovel. The driver lost his patience.

'*Non, monsieur!* This far but no farther. It's one thing to be brave, another to be stupid. It's already six o'clock and it's getting dark. Soon the bears will be coming down to grab some sheep and they don't have a very friendly disposition. We must turn back.'

But Steines was obsessed. He *had* to get to the top, and straight away. The driver was stunned.

'But it's 12km over to Baréges. You can hardly see the road at the moment. What's it going to be like when it's dark?'

Steines couldn't be dissuaded. The driver stared at him, then shrugged. He gave him a few words of advice, told him he'd take the normal route to Baréges and wait for him on the other side, and then they parted.

Lonely now, Steines walked on. His commitment lasted a kilometre. Then it crept on him these weren't the boulevards of Paris. These were the raw dangerous spaces of a mountain. His coat was good but his patent-leather shoes? And a thin cane instead of a walking stick?

His foolhardiness came home with a literal chill. He pressed on for a moment, then hesitated as a tumble of stones fell to the track. A bear? No, a shepherd. Steines gasped in relief, his breath clouding between them. He reached in his pocket, pushed a sovereign into the man's hand and begged him to take him to the top.

They walked through the darkness until the track flattened and started to drop. The shepherd wished him luck, turned and walked back to his flock. Again Steines was alone. The night fell quickly and thickly, as happens in the south, and the mountain cast inky shadows in the moonlight. The thin sticks that marked the path disappeared.

Steines felt panic rise. He heard the gurgling of a stream and headed towards it, to follow it downstream. And then the snow disappeared from under him. He'd started an avalanche and it swept him down the mountain, throwing him over a small cliff and hurling him several metres into a huge, soft snowdrift. There wasn't much courage left, but there was at least the shovel. He started to dig himself out.

Down in the valley, the driver had already set off the alarm. It was obvious the stubborn journalist would never cope alone and he sent off a rescue party. It found him where he'd collapsed at three in the morning.

Nobody slept in Baréges that night. Everybody wanted to see the crazy man who tried to conquer the Tourmalet in slacks and patent-leather shoes. It may have been madness but they respected him. They cheered as he staggered into the village with his rescuers.

Steines slept for 12 hours at the home of *L'Auto*'s local correspondent. And then he sent a telegram to Desgrange.

NO TROUBLE CROSSING TOURMALET STOP
ROADS SATISFACTORY STOP
NO PROBLEM FOR CYCLISTS STOP STEINES

Far north in Paris, Desgrange knew no better. He pulled the cover off his typewriter and began to write.

'The Tour de France 1910 will be over the Peyresourde, the Aspin, Tourmalet and Aubisque.'

Now there was no going back.

Let's move forward, to the evening of July 21. The day has crossed the four mountains and only 10 riders have crossed the line. The rest were heaped in the *voiture balai*.

Desgrange was home in Paris, complaining of illness – although the Tour itself says he probably had nothing worse than nerves. Officials saved the remainder of his race for him.

'Right!' they said. 'This one time, everyone is allowed to start again in the morning. But just this one time only. Now everyone knows it's possible to conquer the Pyrénées. And Garrigou, who was the only one to get all the way over the Tourmalet without walking, he will receive 100 francs as a special prize.'

Steines was proud and relieved. He'd done it. It had been a success. Spectators had been wild with enthusiasm.

But nobody would ever forget what happened on the Aubisque. The officials had waited longer than they'd ever thought possible. They stood in the thin but surprisingly warm mountain air and worried their riders had rebelled or collapsed or been eaten by bears.

Eventually a regional rider, Lafourcade, pushed his bike towards them. They ran to join him. Where were the others? What had happened to them? Were they safe?

But Lafourcade said nothing. He was too shattered to speak. He pushed on through the dust to the top, climbed wearily back on to his bike and began the rocky descent that Steines had tried to follow earlier in the year.

Another 15 minutes passed. Then another bow-backed hero walked into sight. It was Octave Lapize.

They watched him, remembering Lafourcade's exhaustion. He turned his head as he passed the abashed group.

'Murderers!' he hissed. 'Murderers!'

5

A moustache, poison and blue glasses

Fervent support: Not much escapes the critical or enthusiastic gaze of the knowledgeable crowd at every Tour de France.

A moustache, poison and blue glasses

'It's... all gone... wrong... boss! Look!' Desgrange had watched the race official running towards him with a large piece of paper. Now the official passed it to him.

'They want to lynch Garrigou tomorrow,' he said breathlessly. 'What are we going to do?'

Desgrange held out the poster to read it.

Citizens of Rouen! If I had not been poisoned,
I would be leading the Tour de France today.
You know what to do
when the Tour passes through Rouen tomorrow.
Duboc.

Desgrange frowned. This was not good, whether Paul Duboc was behind it or not. Damn this problem! Now he'd have to ban the riders from accepting meals from strangers. He thought about the previous day's events.

They'd started when the Tour went into the Pyrénées for the second time, in 1911. Gustave Garrigou was the race favourite. It had happened in curious circumstances, after Octave Lapize had been found exhausted in a stream on the Ballon d'Alsace and after some imbecile had brought down Lucien Petit-Breton by walking out in front of the finishing sprint. The dapper little Garrigou now faced his main challenge from Paul Duboc.

Duboc was so skinny that people claimed he 'hasn't once in his life eaten until he was full.' But his thinness was misleading. It made him an excellent climber. He made his move right at the start of the Tourmalet and had a huge lead by the obligatory food stop at the top.

The mountain farmers were crazy about Duboc. They celebrated him in songs and slogans and they carried him about in a golden chair. One of them thrust a water bottle at him and he drained it greedily before getting back on his bike for the descent.

He didn't get far down. The pain hit like lightning and he fell off. He realised in an instant that the water must have been poisoned. Sweat broke out on his forehead, his stomach twisted in violent cramp, and he threw up. For more than an hour he lay and suffered on the mountainside between the Tourmalet and Aubisque. His stomach threw up its contents and then a green bile as it struggled to be rid of the poison. The *voiture balai* was waiting for him.

Duboc refused to get in. He struggled to his feet, forced himself over the Aubisque and ground on to the finish. There a blanket was thrown over his shoulders and he was led off to a hotel for soup. At the same time Desgrange was complaining at the police station. Detectives climbed the mountain next day to find the poisoner. But he'd vanished. Nobody had seen which of the crowd of outstretched hands had held the bottle. Then the rumours began. Garrigou was behind it, or if not him then his manager. Duboc himself didn't believe it – they were friends and colleagues – but the fans were convinced. And they were angry.

They sent Garrigou threats. Crowds stood at the finish every day to menace him. Things became so bad that Desgrange had to find him a bodyguard throughout each stage and at hotels. It prevented violence but it didn't quell the anger. And now the Tour was approaching Rouen, and Rouen was Duboc's home town.

'Boss, what are we going to do?'

The official's worried question brought Desgrange back to the present. He collected himself with a sigh, his moustache vibrated with energy and his thin face took on a sly, almost amused expression.

'First we have to get hold of Duboc,' he said thoughtfully. 'And then we shall have to see what we can do with Garrigou's face before the masses do!'

They found Duboc in a restaurant with his assistants. Desgrange pushed the poster under his nose. Duboc choked on his tiny meal.

'I know nothing about this. I've already told them it was nothing to do with my competitors. This is terrible. Do you think I should leave the race and go to Rouen and try to calm people down?'

It was no answer. Desgrange just wanted to be sure of Garrigou's innocence. He looked across at Garrigou himself, equally pale, sitting at a neighbouring table with his knife and fork moving in automatic rhythm. Garrigou had already heard of the posters and his thoughts were elsewhere. Only that day he'd escaped a man who shouted 'In Rouen... nobody can protect you there!' His eyes filled with tears as he thought about it again and then his hands fell still. Desgrange approached him.

'Gustave, it's not that bad. Come to my room an hour and a half before the start. That's an order.'

The next morning Garrigou knocked at the door at the appointed hour. The editor was in excellent mood. He wouldn't be able to write it straight away but this would be one of his best stories.

'Sit down, Gustave,' he said.

The star sat and as he did so he noticed a man standing nearby with a knife, scissors and other strange things at his side. What on earth was happening?

'Don't worry. We'll make sure even your own mother wouldn't recognise you.'

And then the transformation began. A moustache was glued to his upper lip, he changed into a new vest, was fitted with blue-tinted sunglasses and finally a pair of new shoes were added before he could go looking for his bike which had been painted a different colour!

Desgrange swore the bunch to stay together until beyond Rouen. And it worked. The angry crowd searched for Garrigou in the swirling mass that swept through the city, but Garrigou wasn't to be seen. He hid his fear as well as he could and got through Rouen without trouble. Moments later the crowd learned it had been fooled. Fists and tempers rose. But it was too late.

Garrigou held his lead to the finish. Paul Duboc fought his way, unbelievably, to second place – but it was the nearest he ever came to the top of the podium.

6

Cheers for the old Gaul!

'Le Vieux Gaulois': Eugéne Christophe, repairing his front forks in 1919. The first wearer of the Yellow Jersey, it took over an hour and his dream of winning the Tour ended, as it had in 1913 on the road to Dunkirk and was to do again in 1922.

Cheers for the old Gaul!

The stranger wondered about the party at the end table at Le Vieux Gaulois. He'd entered the little restaurant on the rue du Faubourg Montmartre by chance. He ordered his meal and enjoyed it, and then with increasing amazement watched the group of young people who proclaimed one toast after another. The first confirmed they were celebrating an idol.

'He was the greatest, *Vive Le Vieux Gaulois!*'

'*Oui, vive Christophe!*'

The next: 'Long live the front wheel!'

The second and third wheels followed. And then: 'Cheers for the blacksmith in Ste-Marie-de-Campan!'

'Cheers for the leader's yellow jersey!'

'Cheers for the world's greatest unfortunate!'

The many toasts took their time and the glasses were constantly refilled Their eyes became a little unfocused but still they glowed with adoration, and their voices rose in hefty discussions about bike races. Fists banged on tables, berets began to sit awkwardly, and the conversation sparkled with excitement. They each had their own idol but the greatest of all was Le Vieux Gaulois. Of that there was no doubt. What's more, he'd given his name to the restaurant.

The stranger could no longer control his curiosity.

'Gentlemen,' he said, 'I am mad about bike races. I follow the Tour de France every year. But who is this Vieux Gaulois? He seems to have escaped me, and yet you call him the greatest.'

Astonished laughter rose from the group. The head of the table was fastest to control himself.

'You say that you follow the Tour de France and yet you don't know Eugène Christophe? Shall we tell him who the old man is, so that he can enlighten the people wherever it is that he comes from?'

Mumbles of approval came from the others. Wine was poured for the stranger so that he could follow the story better.

'Well, monsieur,' the head of the table began, '1912 was a terrible year for the Tour. A Belgian won for the first time. A *Belgian!* But then again they all rode together against the Belgian team Alcyon, which also had some good French riders. Things were so bad that Octave Lapize got off his bike and said 'Fight? How? All the Belgians are riding for Defraye and against Alcyon.' And that from the man who'd won the Tour in 1910.

'There was only one man who didn't give up. He was 20 years old and his name was Eugène Christophe. They called him Cri-Cri. And he fought like a man possessed, monsieur. He won the three big Alpine stages and he was the first over the Tourmalet. In fact if the rules hadn't been so idiotic he would have won the whole thing.'

There were fresh murmurs of approval.

'*Règles imbéciles... points ridicules.*'

Their hands reached for their glasses. They'd gone through this before. It had developed through the years, generations even, and it was timed perfectly. The next toast approached rapidly.

The storyteller continued.

'The rules were so completely mad that the Tour de France was won on place points instead of combined time. That was the way it was from 1905 until they changed it in 1912. If it had been combined time, like now, Christophe would surely have won instead of Defraye.' He turned suddenly to his companions. 'What is the worst thing you can call a Belgian?' he challenged.

'A Belgian!' they roared back to much laughter. The old joke never failed.

'Long live the battle against the Belgians!'

It took until the glasses were empty and numerous contented sighs had been expelled for the story to continue. The stranger noticed with surprise that small beer glasses had been placed in front of them.

'You see, on points, Christophe came in second, and he explained the situation to Desgrange, who had already seen the problem. So now come the following year, 1913, it was the combined time that decided the winner and once again it was Christophe against the Belgians. Things were just the same and once again Lapize and his entire team gave up in protest. But a few days later the Alcyon team did the same when Defraye was injured in a terrible crash.

'You see, it was the sixth stage, over the Pyrénées, and Thys was leading ahead of Christophe. That was the order they got to the top of the Tourmalet. Eugène was in stunning shape and everybody expected he'd catch Thys on the Aubisque and then he'd go on and win the Tour. But then he found his front fork had broken!'

The little group became animated again.

'Down with the idiots who can't make strong enough bicycles!' More drinks disappeared in willing gulps. Glasses were refilled equally quickly.

'Eugène stopped, but it was no use. His dream of winning the Tour vanished in that moment. The Tour rules were that he couldn't take a bicycle or any parts from his team-mates or from anybody else. He had to do his repairs himself. Down in the valley he saw a little village and he began to run down to it, carrying his bike. All the other riders passed him. And then finally he reached Ste-Marie-de-Campan.'

The table rose in fresh toast.

'Long live the blacksmith in Ste-Marie-de-Campan!'

'Eugène asked a young girl for help and she took him to Monsieur Lecomte, the blacksmith. Christophe had been a lock maker before he became a cyclist so at least he knew how to handle a forge. He took the fork off the bike and brought it to the anvil.'

Again he turned to the group at the table.

'Who here knows how to repair a fork?'

'No, no,' they said. This was too much. 'People only read newspapers these days. The old crafts are lost.' But they were willing to learn.

'There was an audience. There were people from the village, of course, and there were officials from some of the teams and from the race. They wanted to be sure that Christophe didn't break the rules, you see. He had to do it all himself.

'Well, if you repair something on a forge, the time comes when you have to hold it in one hand and your hammer in the other and you need to operate the bellows to keep the fire good and hot. The blacksmith did his best to help him secretly but the officials spotted him. Finally Eugène had to take the chance and ask a boy to pump air for him while he got on with the job.

'It took four hours to get the bike ready. He put it back together and got ready to ride off. But then came one of the most meaningless penalties in the history of the Tour. An official put his hand on Christophe's arm. 'You know that it's not allowed to have help in making repairs,' he said. 'You have a one-minute penalty.'

'You can imagine, monsieur. Christophe could hardly believe his ears. But his eyes smiled for the first time since his bike collapsed. A bitter smile. 'You're joking!', it seemed to say, 'what difference does another minute make now?'

'Down with meaningless one-minute penalties!'

The third round of beers disappeared. Nobody wanted another. Some were getting to the stage where they wanted to burst into song. Others were on their fifth cigar. The air was thick with smoke, boozy breath and sympathy for the poor Christophe.

'And that's the end of the story?' the stranger asked.

'Certainly not, monsieur. Christophe completes the Tour, but he's unplaced. Maybe he could have won if the old rules had applied and it made no difference how much time he lost, if all that mattered was where he finished on each stage. But what does it matter? Christophe became a legend. Philippe Thys won the Tour, but how many people remember that? All genuine Tour lovers have heard of Le Vieux Gaulois and they know there is a plaque at the smithy in Ste-Marie-de-Campan to celebrate him. And now you know yourself, monsieur.

'But that is not all. Bad luck seldom travels alone. And besides, we haven't yet drunk enough. Listen and hear what happened next...

'What happened to Christophe happened before the first world war. So imagine what the roads were like in 1919, when the war finished. Everything about the 1919 Tour was wrong. It was even Tour number 13. Many of the best riders, like Faber and Lapize, had been killed in the fighting. There were hardly any tyres. Only 11 riders made it to the finish in Paris.

'Old Desgrange got the idea for a jersey to show the crowds who was leading the race. He ordered a dozen jerseys in Paris, all of which he was happy to have in strong, bright colours. As it happened, jerseys were also in short supply after the war and all he could get was half a dozen in bright yellow. And so the *maillot jaune* was born.

'On the evening of July 17, 1919, Christophe wore the first yellow jersey. 'It shows you're the leader and I hope you wear it all the way to Paris', Desgrange told him. After all, there were only six of the 15 stages left. And everything continued until the last but one day. In the hell of the north, the field hit the cobbles.'

'Down with the hell of the north!'

'Suddenly Christophe's front fork breaks again.'

'Down with the awful cycle-makers.'

'Once again he had to make his way to the nearest blacksmith and make his own repairs. This time he didn't have to go so far. But all the same he came third after Lambot, who won for the first time. The time differences were huge again and the *lanterne rouge* was 21 hours behind the winner.

'You'd think that Christophe's bad luck was over, wouldn't you? But no. In 1922, when he was 39, he took the yellow jersey again. But guess what happened, this time on the Galibier in the Alps?'

Everyone leaned backwards, threw out his arms and exclaimed in a sad chorus: 'The front fork broke... he walked down the Galibier... he repaired his bike... and he dropped out of the running.'

'Long live the fighting Gaul!'

'When Christophe was 40, in 1923, Desgrange finally allowed the riders to exchange bikes and parts. Too late for Eugène, of course, but what a cyclist! *Tant pis!* He should have won three Tours but all he came away with was a third and two wins in Bordeaux-Paris, in 1920 and 1921. At least now he's immortal.'

'Long live the immortal Vieux Gaulois!'

The stranger smiled wisely through the haze of smoke, beer and red wine. Poor Christophe. Brave Christophe. Unforgettable Christophe.

'Yes,' he said. 'I'll take him home and tell people about him. And now, gentlemen, it is my round. Another toast for the old Gaul!'

A moustache, poison and blue glasses

7

Death in the afternoon

The first Italian winner: Ottavio Bottecchia on the Col I'Izoard. Winner of 1924 and 1925 Tours this legendary Italian rider, from a poor family of nine children, met with a tragic and mysterious death in 1927.

Death in the afternoon

The quiet of the deathbed was heightened by the ticking of the alarm clock, the laboured breathing of the dying, and the faint moans of his wife. She sat with the cross in her hands and prayed for his soul. May his death be easy after the many good years they'd worked in the vineyard.

It had been a long time since he'd been conscious. She wished he would open his eyes, just briefly, and say something she could remember.

Suddenly he woke with a start.

'Get Father Luigi! It's important!'

His wife calmed him.

'There, there. You've always been meticulous in your confessions. Nothing can be *that* important.'

But it was that important. The man became animated. He couldn't die before this had been settled. His voice was almost normal as he repeated: 'You go and get Father Luigi – now!'

The priest had never doubted this old true man of the church. If he said it was important and urgent to make a confession, then hurry he would. But what could it be? What could there be of his life that they hadn't discussed each day over wine in the creamery, when they explored life, the village and their common passion: cycling. They had marvelled at Gino Bartali and felt proud of the honour he'd brought Italy in 1948, and in France at that. He remembered how they'd cheered in 1924 when Bottecchia became the first Italian to win. To this day, he recalled, Bottecchia and Bartali were still the only Italians to win the Tour.

The room was gloomy despite the white lace tablecloth. The furniture was heavy and dark brown, the photographs faded and small, pictures of women in black dresses and men in the dark suits they wore on special days. Why were they always in black when the day was festive? Why, the clergyman wondered, am I too always in black?

'I am here, Mario', he said quietly to the round restless face, its eyes closed, the moustache impressive. He knew the illness was incurable, that death was just a matter of time. But Mario was strong enough to fight a few days yet.

The wrinkled face opened its eyes, appeared to collect itself and then gathered strength.

'Luigi? Good. Maria, you can go...'

Maria closed the door as she left. And Mario began the story he'd been preparing for many years. He'd learned it by heart, so much so that the father thought it was some sort of play he was acting out. But suddenly it became startlingly real.

'Luigi, I want to tell you about a day many years ago. It had just turned into summer. I had had an argument with Maria. It was about money, of course, because the frost had damaged the vines and our finances weren't good.'

He paused.

'I found a man in my vineyard. He was a cyclist, and his bike had ploughed through several vines before he'd thrown it to one side and sat down to enjoy the sun. He looked to me like one of those people who wander through the vines, ruining everything by pushing into the field to get the bunch that looks tastiest. They have no respect for the hard work of an honest farmer.'

He moaned and closed his eyes. Then, with pain, he continued.

'It was too much for me. How many vines had he ruined? I was angry because he represented all the other people who'd been thieving in my fields. I took a large stone and I crept up on him and I hit him on the head as hard as I could. Father Luigi, believe me, I didn't know what I was doing.'

The old man collapsed into his pillows, exhausted by his effort. His body shook as he took several painful breaths. The priest was stunned and gazed at him wonderingly. So that was what it was all about. And Mario had carried this burden for 21 years. How was it possible?

He remembered that day well. It was June 11, 1927. No one in the village would forget it. Mario ran into the square shouting that a wounded cyclist was in the ditch by his vineyard. He was in a bad way. He must have crashed. There were only two cars in the village and one of them must take him to the hospital in Genoa. It had been a shock for Luigi when the man died and he found he'd been Ottavio Bottecchia.

Mario threw himself to one side of the bed with a start. His eyes were lit with the anxiety he'd felt that day. He pulled himself back together and continued the confession he'd prepared for so many years.

'Bottecchia. Ottavio Bottecchia. It was after I'd hit him that I saw who he was. My... your... idol. With blood all over his face, that face that had been dried by the wind and thinned by tough races and hard training. I remember those eyes, staring out of those dark holes, lifeless.'

Mario was fading. He closed his eyes to gather more strength.

Father Luigi once again remembered. They'd been so irritated that Italy talked only of Girardengo. Always Girardengo, the winner of every Italian championship from 1914 to 1925 and five times the winner of the Giro. How they'd tired of him. And only once had the man tried the Tour de France, and then without success, where he could really have shown how great he was.

He smiled suddenly when he thought of the 1923 Tour de France. The intolerable Pélissier brothers had taken an unknown Italian on to their Automoto team and he quickly became famous. He won the stage into Cherbourg and was second overall. If Bottecchia had been allowed to attack his own team leader, he and not Pélissier would have won the Tour. And Pélissier had said that Bottecchia could win the next year.

What a dream! Imagine an Italian winning for the first time.

From the bed, Mario gasped: 'Luigi, do you remember he led from start to finish?'

Luigi got up suddenly, and he was furious. Was this not his best friend lying there, confessing that he'd murdered the man who was destined to destroy Girardengo and who should have become champion of the world? And all for a few grapes?

'How could you do that to our idol? To our dream of an Italian victory in the Tour?'

The old man lifted himself on an elbow.

'Stop! You are the priest. You are supposed to forgive, not to condemn.'

Luigi blushed.

'I became a murderer,' Mario gasped. 'My anger overtook me. I couldn't control myself over a couple of vines. Every time a Frenchman wins the Tour de France, it's like a knife stabbing my heart. But I beg for your forgiveness.'

Father Luigi was still shocked. But he collected himself and whispered to his dying friend.

'Don't worry. If I even for a moment condemned your terrible action, it is only because I too am a weak human who loves cycling stars. But God does not ride a bike. He sees into your heart, and it is pure. Everyone has a moment in his life when he's so enraged that he could kill, and he is unfortunate who, in that one moment, actually has the opportunity to do so.'

'Father Luigi,' Mario said, more relaxed now. 'You must reveal this once I am dead, but you must also say that the first sinner that day was Bottecchia. He had no respect for me and my vineyard. No matter how many times he'd won the Tour, he should still have respected my vines.'

He asked for Maria and his face became peaceful as he said a last farewell. Now he was at peace with his god, his sport and his heroes.

So, Bottecchia was killed in a vineyard on June 11, 1927. But more than that we will never know. Many claim to know the truth, but the mystery remains unsolved. There was indeed a deathbed confession by an old peasant in 1948. For me, it's the most fascinating explanation and I like to believe it's true.

8

Two kisses for a German

Overcome by a kiss: Octave Lapize in 1910! The little Parisian, nicknamed 'Curly', was one of cycling's greatest champions, for as well as the Tour de France, he won the gruelling Paris-Roubaix classic three-times, and so the winner over the cobblestones of northern France, would be the first over the rough mule and cart tracks of the Preyénées, as the Aspin, Peyresourde and Tourmalet, were climbed for the first time.

Two kisses for a German

There has been an important change in the Tour de France. I have given it a lot of study, and it's this: the Tour de France kissing girls. I, a German professor, would like to address you tonight in my role as my country's foremost expert on kissing.

Ladies and gentlemen, as you know, the Tour de France is an expression of the immoral French culture. There is no other country in which the entire population goes so completely amok over a couple of hundred cyclists who spend a month pedalling away. On top of this, they adore these cyclists so much that they use one of their greatest expressions of adulation – kissing.

It has been like this since the beginning in 1903. It soon became an honour to be the one who celebrated the winner of each stage with hugs and kisses. Women, ladies and gentlemen, would all but fight over it. Often it was the wife of the mayor or a local businessmen. They would admire the beautiful, determined eyes, the well-trained legs and the nice bums, and then threaten their husbands into giving them this honour.

Sometimes not all went well. Observe this picture of 1910. The winner is Octave Lapize. He is rendered defenceless by his bike, his bouquets of flowers, and cramp. And here you see him being overwhelmed by the kisses of a very solid female with stiff petticoats, feathers in her hair, and a cleavage into which the poor man is in danger of disappearing.

It is altogether a violent scene, but the organisers realise it makes good advertising. So they take it a stage further and insist, for the safety of the riders and the good of the race, that the kissing is done by the local beauty queen.

Now beauty, ladies and gentlemen, is very variable. There are many towns so small that they don't contain any real beauties. And not all cyclists are desirable either. Consider my next exhibit. This is a picture from Les Sables-d'Olonne on the Atlantic coast, in 1928. Observe the two short-skirted but none-too-friendly local beauties alongside Nicolas Frantz. He is the winner of the day and later of the Tour. Look at his face. My question is: Is that the face of a winner?

Look at the women, my friends. Note the expression on their faces. They are obliged to kiss him. And they have just realised that a stage winner moments after winning is anything but gorgeous. He sweats, he is covered in mud, and even though he is about to put on another jersey, it is not difficult to see that he should have had a bath and brushed his teeth, *nicht wahr?*

Kissing girls is popular. The spectators love to see it and the photographers would much rather immortalise a winner with a pretty girl than with his bicycle. The girls were vital for the sponsors when television came.

You do not simply become a kissing girl these days. The Tour de France is no longer interested in mayors' wives and local pageant queens. These days a kissing girl must speak several languages, be beautiful and also fit enough to kiss her way round France without collapsing of tiredness. These girls are picked at interviews from hundreds who apply.

Perhaps there is also a practical test. Maybe there is a sort of kissing audition. I have no idea. But most of these girls have a natural ability. I can confirm this, ladies and gentlemen, from my own experience.

Kissing blossoms around the Tour. A cyclist may be so lucky as to get a spontaneous kiss from an admirer as he arrives to sign in for the day's stage. It has been known for a Frenchwoman to forget herself so much when a national hero crosses the line that she will plonk a spontaneous smacker on the cheek of the man next to her.

Sometimes the kissing can change the race. I would like to continue my lecture now by telling you about the two kisses that helped my compatriot Erich Bautz towards a remarkable achievement in 1937.

After impressive efforts, not least in the mountains, Erich Bautz had become a professional in 1934. His career had not lived up to expectations and it was only in 1937 that he first challenged himself in the world's hardest race. Nevertheless he was the new German champion when he arrived in Paris for the start.

He had passed through Customs simply by uttering the words 'Tour de France'. As fit as they had ever been, what they most wanted was a good night on the town and a kiss from a French coquette. *Wunderbar, nein?*

But their director was merciless.

'Go to bed!' he ordered. 'Just tell yourself you're on a desert island where there's nothing to do. A taste of the night life is waiting for you but only when we're back in Paris. And then we'll see if you've got the energy for it!'

Bautz slept badly, worried about the race. There was the usual restlessness at the start next morning. He sought out Thierbach, a German who'd completed several Tours, and they discussed the personalities already present.

'They only come here to be seen,' Thierbach explained. 'If they want to be photographed with you, it's only so they can get into the papers themselves. Don't kid yourself it's because they know or care about you.'

And then Josephine Baker came up to our team. She was no longer just an exotic black dancer in a banana skirt; she had won world renown as a cabaret singer. Her song, *J'ai deux amours – mon pays et Paris* (I have two loves – my country and Paris) was perfect for the occasion.

A journalist pointed out the German champion and Josephine floated over the cobblestones in a cloud of perfume to plant a graceful kiss on Bautz's cheek. The German blushed.

'Don't get any funny ideas,' Thierbach warned him. 'You'll have to win a stage if you want any more kisses.'

Bautz did indeed want another kiss, and preferably where there'd be a lot of other Germans to see. It would have to be on the fourth stage, from Metz to Belfort. That would take them 1,250 metres high on the Ballon d'Alsace. And the Ballon is in a part of France that was once German. The crowds, his crowds, would be out to see him.

Early in the stage the French rider Carini was allowed to build a lead of 11 minutes. For a long time nobody chased. And then everything happened at once. Small groups, large groups, they chased, merge, split and chased again. Suddenly Bautz accelerated. He had good legs and he put plenty of space between himself and the field. He was relaxed because he'd been taking it easy in the middle of the bunch while Carini was been fighting alone in the baking sun.

Smile please:
The kissing girls were
sometimes too shy!

He passed the Italian easily on the 9km climb. Friendly officials on motorbikes made it easier by telling him how far ahead he was of Carini and the bunch. Three minutes, they told him, and more than ten on the yellow jersey. At the start Bautz was in only 14th place. Now he realised he could take the yellow jersey.

The crowds cheered and sprayed him from garden hoses and bottles. He could hardly move for journalists and photographers as he crossed the line. He had taken the yellow jersey.

She was waiting there, the beauty queen of Belfort. And it was a big enough town that they really could choose the prettiest. She had clearly practised, and she gave Erich Bautz a kiss. It was one he'd never forget. And it was clear that she, too, would always remember.

She probably also never forgot that the yellow jersey, *her* yellow jersey, held the lead for three days. He lost it with three punctures on the Galibier. But he did win another stage before the race ended. And with it another kiss.

And that, *dames und herren*, concludes my lecture this evening.

9

King René

A French hero:
René Vietto (second
from left) poses
with some of his
fans. Unfortunately
the lovable former
lift-boy never won
the Tour. Second
in 1939 he returned
again in 1947 to
make yet more
sacrifices for
his team.

King René

We want a bedtime story! We want a bedtime story! 'Come on, children – it's late and I have to go back to the others. Do you really think your parents invited me just so that I would sit here telling you my stories all night?'

'Oh, grandad. *Your* stories are the best of all. You know so many. That one about the old Gaulois, the one about the cannibal, and the one about King René. That's the best of all. Please?'

Two pairs of begging eyes were more than I could resist. And I love that story too.

'But you know it by heart. What about another one, maybe about Robin Hood?'

'No, grandad. It's always so exciting. René's story gives us goose bumps. Every night I dream that this time he will succeed, and...'

'All right, all right – you win...'

'Once upon a time there was a lift boy in a huge and luxurious hotel in Cannes, alongside the glittering Mediterranean. It was one of those hotels where millionaires spend their holidays and people point if you turn up in a Bentley and not a Rolls-Royce. The lift boy's name was René Vietto. He was a slender, black-headed youngster and the guests liked him. They tipped him generously and asked him about his passion, which was cycling. He used to go out in his spare time and train and dream of riding the Tour de France. Eventually he became so good that he left his job and in 1934 he was picked for the French national squad for the Tour. The selectors thought he may not be the best but he was good and he'd be loyal to the team captain.'

'His captain was Tonin, Antonin Magne, who was the star of all cycling, and René admired and respected him. Tonin's word was law and René trained desperately to prove himself worthy of being chosen.'

'But it was obvious when the race started that the best rider of all was René. Magne captured the yellow jersey according to plan but in the Alps René won first in Grenoble and then in Digne. Cannes was on its toes to hail its lift boy when the stage finished there, and René obliged by breaking away and winning far ahead of the others. There was never a celebration like there was in Cannes that day.'

'And he could have won the whole Tour, couldn't he, grandad?'

'You bet he could. And lots of people told him so when the race arrived in the Pyrénées. It was only the second year there'd been a mountain competition and for the first time there was a bonus for the first rider over the highest peaks. Vietto was becoming a king, a mountain king, and thousands of people were soon his fans right across France.'

'Magne is exhausted,' they said. 'King René is going to win in the Pyrénées.' And then Magne crashed going down the col de Puymorens on the first day in the Pyrénées. René rushed to his rescue. Tonin was only slightly hurt but his front wheel had crumpled and his main rival, the Italian Martano, had got away.'

'Vietto shouted 'Here, take my wheel!' and Magne fought to catch Martano while Vietto waited for the service car. Magne was just 28 seconds down by the finish and he'd saved his yellow jersey. But the young mountain king was weeping. He'd dreamed of standing on the podium with his idol and leader.'

'The next day, though, his spirits rose again. He attacked early, led over the col de Porte, and he was in the front group climbing the col d'Aspet when Magne was again hit by trouble. His back tyre had a slow puncture. He dropped back discreetly, hoping the Italians wouldn't notice and attack. Of Magne's team-mates, only Vietto noticed and he dropped back as well. But Magne didn't appear.'

'Now, Vietto could have won the Tour himself. But he didn't consider it. He was worried about France and his leader. He turned round and rode back 500 metres to find Magne sitting in a ditch, holding his wheel. What had happened to the service car? Once again King René gave him his wheel. Again Magne set off after Martano, who by then had worked out what was going on and was doing his best to finalise matters. It took 30km to catch him and Magne's yellow jersey was never threatened again.'

'Vietto lost half an hour that day and he never came close to the podium even though he left the rest on the Tourmalet and Aubisque and won the mountain competition. Half of France hailed his loyalty, the other half grieved for his missing victory. Vietto and Magne fans determined to know which was the better decided only the next year could settle it.'

'But the Tour of 1935 was ugly. The favourites fell and left the race one by one. The Spanish rider Cepeda died after a crash on the Galibier, the Tour's first fatality. Stages were haunted day after day by pouring rain. Roads washed away. Vietto won a mountain stage but he was always in the wrong place when crashes split the field. Magne was among those who quit after a fall. Romain Maes, though, had a lucky touch and led from start to finish – and what do we call that, children?'

'*La course en tête*, grandad! That's the only French you ever taught us.'

'Well done. Now on to 1936. King René was still only 22, but alas his knee was injured. He needed an operation and he almost had to give up cycling. And he had other problems as well. He trusted people too much and he let a charlatan take care of his money. Well, maybe the man just made poor investments, or perhaps he robbed Vietto. Whichever it was, he lost all his money and he didn't understand how.'

'He couldn't live without cycling. The yellow jersey was always in his dreams even though he had to sit out in 1937 and 1938. In 1939, there were more places than usual for French riders. The Italians and Germans stayed at home because of the politics that led to world war, and Spain was fighting a civil war. There was an extra Belgian team to make up numbers and there were several French regional teams as usual.'

'Vietto made the Southeast-Mediterranean team. And it was a surprise when he took the yellow jersey just before the Pyrénées because climbers don't usually distinguish themselves on the flat of western France. Vietto wanted to keep the jersey. He had injections in his knee every evening and he told journalists in Pau: 'I'm going to conquer the Aubisque, Aspin and Tourmalet with just one leg, and nobody will rob me of the yellow jersey.'

'The stage was a mixture of wind, fog, rain and ice storms. It was catastrophic for a painful knee and Maes had almost made up Vietto's lead by Toulouse. But Vietto fought on. He defended his jersey for nine days and now came the Izoard. France held its breath. Governments could overturn and presidents be murdered in such turbulent times with nobody noticing and France concentrated instead on Vietto.'

'The first radio reports told how he was riding as though it were still 1934 and both his knees were intact. But then came the endless Izoard and Vietto had to give in when Maes started his final attack. The Belgian's back wheel pulled away and before long his tormentor had vanished. Vietto had to summon all his strength merely to survive, finishing almost half an hour behind Maes. The Belgian won the Tour that day but France acclaimed not him but its hero. Vietto was second and he and not the winner got the louder applause when they climbed to the podium in Paris.'

'Four weeks later, Vietto was in a trench. War had broken out and it seemed there may never be another Tour. Luckily it wasn't true.'

For a moment the story was interrupted.

'What's going on? You can't keep grandad here this long. We want to see him as well when he's here...'

'Yes, yes, mum, but he's just telling us about King René and we're getting to the best bit, where he gets so angry and throws his jersey into the official's face. *Please* let him carry on! Make him! Why don't you listen as well?' So she sat, put an arm round her children, and listened.

I carried on.

'It was too soon, really, to restart the Tour in 1947. The roads were bad and the economy was in ruins. Things were rationed and it was a job just to get food for the riders. Not to mention petrol. It was so hard to get it in remote places that the organisers even bought their own tanker.'

'The Tour de France is the symbol of France, though. If anybody ever doubted it, it was proved now. Everybody made sure there would be a Tour, to show that maybe France wasn't well but it was fighting back to its feet. And unbelievably, King René was still there, a symbol of the fighting French. He was 33, he'd had three knee operations, and still he fought for the yellow jersey. He broke away alone for 130 kilometres in the second stage, from Lille to Brussels, and he got it.'

'The French were gasping in the shade outside their open windows in an unbearably hot summer as they listened to the radios inside the house. Vietto kept the jersey one day, another day, but then after seven days he had to give it up.'

'And yet King René not only won the stage but got the yellow jersey back as well in one of the Alp stages finishing at Digne. And the Pyrénées didn't crack him either.'

'There were only three days left but everybody knew he wouldn't stay the *maillot jaune* because a long time-trial came just before the end. And Vietto was a climber, not a time-triallist. He was close to collapse and he could stick on a wheel, France reasoned, but he'd never be able to ride alone.'

'They prayed for a miracle. Vietto ordered a yellow jersey of pure silk from a factory in Lyon. It may be against the rules but it would be lighter and more aerodynamic. He got the lightest tyres and decided to ride with neither cap nor glasses. He was angry with the organisers, convinced they'd put the time-trial near the end to rob him of victory.'

'Unfortunately, there was no happy ending. King René fought his last battle and lost. An official told him he'd lose 10 seconds for his illegal jersey. It was as small as it was petty and it reminded him of Le Vieux Gaulois in 1913. His dream was crushed and he turned on the official and shouted: 'You can't do this to me!'

'He tore off the jersey and threw it at the official's feet. 'Here, take the jersey and dry your feet on it. I'll take the first train back to Cannes. Nothing can make me change my mind.'

'A quiet voice, itself a national symbol, intervened. It was the radio reporter Georges Briquet. 'In the name of your country, I beg you not to quit,' he urged. People at home could hear it all on their radios. They begged Vietto to change his mind. But no.

'The organisers are crooks and they've stolen my yellow jersey,' he raged. 'I'll leave straight away.' And he packed his case and carried it into the lobby of the hotel where he was supposed to sleep. But there were still hours before the train to Cannes would leave at 11.00pm and an official quietly carried the case back to his room. Vietto saw it and brought it back.'

'This happened several times, but at 11pm Vietto wasn't on his train. He rode on to Paris and finished third, taking his place on the podium to greater cheers than the winner and runner-up.'

'But we mustn't forget that the winner deserved his cheers as well. He'd have been the story of the Tour if it hadn't been for René. He was poor and he was newly married, and when he left for the Tour he promised his wife: 'I've got no dowry for you but I'll bring you first prize.'

'He rode well but it didn't look as though he'd keep his promise. First Vietto and then the Italian Pierre Brambilla held the yellow jersey. But he took Brambilla by surprise on the last stage and attacked 140km from the finish. Brambilla suffered for his Italian name and his snooty ways. The war was still a painful memory. It was tradition never to attack the leader on the last day but nobody would help him respond.'

'Jean Robic carried home 500,000 francs – a large sum – and gave them to his wife. He and Jan Janssen in 1968 are still the only riders to have stood in yellow in Paris without riding a metre in the *maillot jaune*.'

The little boy gasped.

'What a shame for brave King René,' he said.

The little girl whispered: 'So romantic, though. Robic's wife must have been very happy and grateful.'

'Now,' said their mother, 'you must go to sleep now. Grandad is really much too kind. You trick him every single time he's here to tell you stories that are much too long. Sweet dreams!'

A moustache, poison and blue glasses

10

Bartalists, Coppists and Il Campionissimo

The 'Lion of Tuscany': Gino Bartali riding over the terrifying Alpine mountain pass, the Col d'Izoard. Bartali would win the Tour in 1938, just before the war, and then claim another victory an incredible ten years later.

Bartalists, Coppists and Il Campionissimo

If the second world war saved France from anything, it was a string of Italian victories in the Tour. The race simply couldn't be held.

Italian cycling has developed through a stream of exceptional cyclists. The greatest becomes the *campionissimo*, the champion of champions. Many have held the title: Costante Girardengo, for instance, undefeated Italian champion from 1914 to 1925; and his successor, Alfredo Binda, who won the next four years. Both won the Giro d'Italia, Milan-San Remo and other great Italian races. But whereas Girardengo tried the Tour de France only in 1914, and then unsuccessfully, Binda captained Italy after Henri Desgrange abolished trade teams to be rid of the factory bosses and to appeal to national rivalry.

Binda soon found what team cycling meant. At least against the French. They were simply better at it and they left him far behind, with 'just' two stage wins in the Pyrénées. It was disheartening. But not for long. Italy was soon to have not one but two *campionissimo*, men who filled the papers and split the nation. Just as in 1960s Britain it was impossible to like both the Beatles and the Rolling Stones, so in Italy you were for Gino Bartali or Fausto Coppi. You couldn't back both.

Bartali came first. His first yellow jersey came at the start of the mountains stages in 1937. Italy was delighted. Unfortunately Bartali lost it again next day when he fell off a narrow wooden bridge and into a stream. The cuts and bruises didn't stop him finishing the stage but he retired next day.

In 1938 he promised Italian journalists he'd win. They soon scoffed. He rode a quiet race and there was little sign it would happen. But Bartali had a manager who knew what he was talking about – the old man Girardengo. He insisted his crumple-faced star would find inspiration in the Pyrénées and then win in the Alps. The journalists waited.

Bartali was a religious obsessive. He prayed frequently and never ate without a religious statuette on the table. His fans called him 'Bartali the Pious'. A Tour never passed Lourdes, the shrine of revelation, without Bartali taking the chance to touch the wall of the holy cave and be blessed.

Maybe it was there, at the foot of the Pyrénées, that he gained his strength for the Alps. He broke away between Digne and Briançon and left his chasers a staggering 17 minutes behind on the 2,631 metres of the col de l'Izoard. Thousands of Italians had crossed the border on Girardengo's promise and they burst like fireworks as he rode alone into Briançon.

They cheered for Bartali, they cheered for *Il Duce*, Mussolini, and they cheered for Italy. Their hero vanished into a street-wide throng of fanatics struggling to touch him, squeeze him, gain something of his magic. The Italian general Antonelli shouted: 'Don't touch him... don't touch him! Bartali is God himself!'

Just as he prayed at Lourdes, Bartali took his victory wreath and laid it at the altar of Nôtre Dame. He clasped his medallion of the holy Thérèse and prayed again. No other athlete was as regularly received by the Pope as this builder's son from Florence.

Maybe that explains the strange calm around him. He never gave himself away. Reporters tried, oh how they tried, but they never breached the almost mystical facade. His face was expressionless, identical in victory and defeat. His broken nose made him look like a boxer, but beyond that there was nothing to read but unsmiling sadness or indifference. Except you couldn't even tell if he was sad or indifferent.

Bartali was a blank on which dreaming Italians could paint the virtues and motives they chose. He could be whatever they wanted him to be. Above all, he could be an antidote to Fausto Coppi.

Coppi was just a kid when he won a race for unlicensed riders near his home in Castellania. His prize was 20 lira and a sausage. He got a shock the first time he lined up with the 'real' racers. There with him was Bartali. Coppi didn't win but he did impress Bartali enough to be asked to work with him in the break. And he was impressive enough, too, for the leading Legnano team to offer him a contract.

It was Bartali who later took the credit for discovering Coppi. But then again so did others. But it was Giuseppe 'Biagio' Cavanna who wrote to Eberardo Pavesi at Legnano to alert him to Coppi's arrival, and it was a furious Cavanna who demanded

'il campionissmo':
The glorious
riding style of
Fausto Coppi

that Coppi break a local contract he'd just signed with none other than Costante Girardengo – to whom, amusingly, Coppi had once delivered salami as a butcher's boy and not liked him at all.

So who was this man Cavanna who guided Coppi's career? The answer is that he was a masseur who became a legend when he became blind and talked of knowing all there was to know of his champion merely by touch. Cavanna insisted that Coppi's colossal lungs and his unusually long legs were ideal for cycling. And he was right.

Coppi, though, was frail. Just as boxers have glass jaws, so Coppi had brittle bones. You had only to blow to break them. He even broke an ankle running for a bus at 19. Two years later he broke a collarbone while he was training on the Vigorelli track in Milan. He broke another when he came back from being a prisoner-of-war, then his pelvis in 1950 and then a collarbone again. It was a miracle he had both the health and the time to race at the top.

The war hadn't reached Italy in 1941 when Coppi won Milan-San Remo. It had by November 7, 1942, though, and Coppi broke the hour record in Milan the night after a terrible air raid and despite sirens before and after his ride. His 45.891km survived until Jacques Anquetil bettered it in 1956, by which time both training and bikes were vastly better.

Coppi won the Italian championship in 1942 even after puncturing four minutes behind the two leaders. Legend says Bartali finally sensed that day that Coppi was a threat to his status and popularity.

It took until the end of the war to see if he was right. Coppi became a prisoner in Tunisia and came back to Italy only in the war's last months. The RAF learned from the newspapers whom they had as prisoner and let him race again provided he went no further north than Rome. He was a success despite mild malaria.

Peace gave Bartali the chance to put this 'skinned cat', as he described him, in his place. He predicted before the 1946 Milan-San Remo that 'towards Turchino I will ride so that Coppi screams for his mother.' He never got the chance. Coppi was long gone before Bartali got there. He won by 14 minutes, 24 minutes in front of Bartali.

Still Gino was the more popular. Coppi won the world and Italian pursuit championships in 1947 but he was too mortal for most Italians. They scoffed at his fragile bones and his fancy modern training. By contrast, Bartali was untouchable. He was in the hands of divine powers, he spoke to angels in the mountains.

And then Bartali went to the Tour de France in 1948. He was *Il Vecchio*, the Old One. Free from Coppi, he was invincible. He sprinted to victory on the first stage and then said that he'd follow the orders of his manager, Alfredo Binda, not to defend his yellow jersey. He was 12th, with 20 minutes on the new French hope, Louison Bobet, when he went to pray once more at Lourdes. Perhaps he was asking for help in the Alps.

Rain, sleet and snow fell on the Izoard. The higher Bartali got, the worse it became. Ice skimmed the road. He climbed forcefully, going up in the gears as the others fought for lower ones. Below him, the rest began to suffer. And then Bartali himself weakened. He'd forgotten his food. His strength was going.

It was then that closeness to heaven helped him. Spectators usually do no more than cheer and wave flags. But now here was a man offering the bizarre treat of three bananas. Bartali ate them.

'They saved my Tour,' he said. Three bananas had brought him within a minute of the yellow jersey. The next day would count.

Unfortunately it dawned still worse. Hail and snow fell between Briançon and Aix-les-Bains. Bobet tried a surprise attack but Bartali came back. Bobet tried again when the Italian punctured but Bartali waited for the chasers and rejoined with them.

The day was a battle between two men. And Bartali finally broke Bobet on the col de Porte. The Frenchman bowed and surrendered 10 minutes. They turned the Tour into a victory parade. Bartali won again in Lausanne the next day and then once more in Liège. In all he took seven stages. And yet still Binda claimed: 'If I had been Bobet's manager, he would have won.'

Bartali didn't care. He returned to Italy in triumph. Coppi soon realised that people forgot when Bartali rode badly. When Bartali rode well, everyone went mad with delight. But when Coppi rode well, it was expected and fine. Yet one bad ride and he was criticised harshly. And by the way, they pointed out, Coppi hadn't ridden the Tour de France.

So why hadn't he? Was he afraid? Was he scared he couldn't come anywhere close to Bartali? Huh!

The Bartalists and Coppists were at war, with fists as well as words. It got worse after the scandal at the world championship in Valkenburg in southern Holland. Coppi and Bartali rode like Siamese twins. They watched each other so closely that the rest of the field passed and left them 10 minutes behind. The crowd jeered as they passed the finish line and retired. Childish! Ridiculous! But the papers were blaming Coppi and not Bartali.

Coppi and Bartali were together in the 1949 Tour team. It was an unhappy partnership; they were archenemies with different sponsors. Binda persuaded them not to attack each other, thinking it a great tactical achievement, but the result was that the Frenchman Marinello took 18 minutes out of them and became the *maillot jaune*. On the fifth stage, Coppi attacked, Marinello went with him, their bikes touched and they crashed. Marinello jumped back but Coppi had to wait six minutes for Binda and the Italian car. He was very, very angry. He wanted to give up. Binda turned to abuse.

'So you want to hand the Tour to Gino, then, you fool?' he shouted, ignoring his non-aggression pact. 'Get back on your bike.'

Coppi got back on but he'd lost his spirit. He lost another 20 minutes even with three team-mates. The peace treaty survived Coppi's constant moaning. But then he won the time-trial outstandingly and his morale returned. Binda let him attack the French in the Pyrénées. Coppi hunched his back and increased his lead over the field on the col d'Aspin until equipment problems hit him and he had to settle for third.

The two Italians outclassed the rest on the Izoard. Bartali was in bargaining mood. He pleaded just before the finish: 'It's my birthday today. Let me win in Briançon. I can already tell that this is going to be your Tour.' Coppi let Bartali win and the Pious finished the day with a minute and 22 seconds on his rival.

Bartali had fresh courage next day. He didn't want it to become Coppi's Tour immediately. He knew he'd win the Tour if he could lead at the end of the day, the last of the hard mountain stages. And he attacked. The big names weren't going to have him grabbing the Tour and they lined up to catch him. The bunch passed into Italy, over the Little St Bernard, and the crowd erupted along the hairpins as Coppi and Bartali went away together.

Bartali punctured. The anti-warfare agreement made Coppi hesitate, anxiety gnawing his insides. And then Binda pulled alongside and yelled: 'Go! Gino's lost five minutes. The French are attacking. Just go!'

And Coppi went. He increased his lead on the descent, held it on the 40km to the finish, and took the yellow jersey. Nothing could shake him. Day by day he increased his lead, winning the sprint on the last but one stage, and finishing 15 minutes ahead of Bartali overall. Both men were *campionissimi* but Coppi was the greater. For the first time, a man had won both the Giro and the Tour in the same year.

Bartali won Milan-San Remo next year. It made the atmosphere electric for the Giro, but not for long because Coppi crashed and broke his pelvis in the early stages. Bartali was no longer young enough by 1951 to threaten the best. Coppi was still mourning his brother Serse, who'd died in another race. He was persuaded to ride the Tour anyway and finished 10th to Hugo Koblet of Switzerland.

He was back in superb shape for 1952. He won the Giro in front of Bartali and that, rumours said, is why Koblet and Bobet withdrew from the Tour. But Coppi had problems all the same. Bartali clung to Coppi's wheel for day after day and the atmosphere was so tense after four days that Coppi left his team-mates and found his own accommodation.

On some stages, though, legs and not tactics were needed. Coppi was invincible in the first time trial – Bartali was 21st – and two days later he pulverised everyone on the first mountain stage. Coppi soared over five mountains of more than 2,000m, had ten minutes on Bartali by the end of the day and was wearing the yellow jersey. Look at Coppi's career and you'll see he was never caught after breaking away alone, except after accidents and mechanical failures.

Il Vecchio lost the will to fight and two days later gave Coppi his wheel after his rival had punctured.

It soon became clear how unbeatable Coppi was. The organisers increased the money for second place to give the others something to race for. He was so strong in 1953 that the Tour – which still picked the teams itself – decided not to ask him. Instead he won the world road championship later that year in Lugano, speeding down the finishing straight past banners advertising Bartali's new Chianti wine. Coppists claimed Bartali bought the space to annoy Coppi. Bartalists denied it. Whatever the truth, Coppi finished seven minutes ahead of the silver medallist and ten minutes before the rest.

He never rode another Tour and never again had a major success. Cycling had made him wealthy but crashes and illness had affected his career. But it was his love of Giulia Locatelli that damned him. Coppi had a wife, Bruna; Giulia was married to a doctor.

Today it would make a good tabloid story but little more. Then, divorce was unacceptable and in Italy above all. Giulia's husband pursued them and the police raided in case Coppi and his woman in white – the title her white coat gave her before her name was known – were sharing a bed. The Vatican, so keen on Bartali, refused to bless the peloton while Coppi was part of it. Giulia's son had to be born abroad to ensure that Coppi and not, as Italian law would assume, Giulia's husband became the registered father.

Bartali rode his last Tour in 1953, coming 11th. Coppi raced on but his health and results deteriorated. Maybe the decline made Bartali's last years easier. Bartali formed his own team and offered Coppi a contract to ride his last year as a 40-year-old and to work with the younger riders. But the collaboration never happened. Coppi went on a racing and hunting trip to Africa in December 1959 and on his return fell ill. Tragically, the Doctors missed the diagnosis of malaria. He died on January 2, 1960. Italy, which had loved and then scorned him, entered a long period of mourning.

A moustache, poison and blue glasses

11

The man who went the wrong way

Refreshment stop: Local café owners often welcomed the Tour riders with food and drink. Here the ever popular Raymond 'Pou Pou' Poulidor (centre) with his Mercier team-mates take a pit-stop at Amiens.

The man who went the wrong way

July 28, 1951, is a boiling hot day. The Tour can think only of water. Something cold to drink; a dip in a town square fountain; a shower from a roadside hose. Stage 13 beside the glittering azure of the Mediterranean from Perpignan to Nîmes is hot indeed. The breeze from the sea does nothing to make the air fresher; it turns it instead into a heat haze which makes the sun pale and turns the air into a pulsating desert mirage. There's no mercy for cyclists.

For all but one team, that is. The North Africans have yet to make a mark but they're at home in this heat. And so, with 200km to go, Marcel Molines and Abdel-Khader Zaaf make a move. Nobody cares. The two are far behind in the standings and there's a long, long way to the finish.

They canter along for hours, picking up 20 minutes on the bunch. Sensationally, that could take Zaaf into the yellow jersey. An amazed audience cheers as they appear in dust clouds so far ahead of riders grateful for a cease-fire.

Zaaf is too excited to drink and he begins to zigzag 20km from the finish, close to collapse. He grabs a bottle from a spectator and drinks in one long, greedy gulp. But it doesn't help. He wobbles even more and eventually an official halts him. He tries once more but this time Zaaf falls from his bike and onlookers pull him to the shadow of a tree, where he falls asleep.

Molines, meanwhile, pushes on and gets his victory in Nîmes. Back down the road, Abdel-Khader Zaaf is recovering slowly. He wakes, stares in disbelief for several seconds at the many people staring back, climbs back on his bike – and sets off the way he's come. It's too much for the spectators and they call an ambulance to take him to Nîmes.

The bottle was white wine. Zaaf, a Muslim, had never drunk alcohol. Exhaustion, dehydration and alcohol made him drunk. He was inconsolable. He'd ridden a superb stage and yet he was out of the race. He asked officials if he could cover the missing 20km ahead of the next day's stage, but they turned him down.

Well, Molines may have won but Zaaf became a celebrity. Every race wanted him when the Tour finished. His fee rose from 200 to 2,000 francs and he made a small fortune that summer.

And then he disappeared. He vanished in Algeria between two races and couldn't be found. Many tried but before long they forgot about him.

Until January 27, 1982. Then he arrived in Paris for an eye operation, some time around his 65th birthday. An old fan recognised him and soon journalists were crowding round him to fill in the missing years.

On that night in Algeria in 1951, it seemed, there was a knock at the door soon after dinner. A soldier asked Zaaf to follow him for a check on his papers. Algeria was to an extent self-governing but ultimately still under French rule. Violence was frequent. Zaaf explained with irritation that he had only just returned from a race in Brittany, that he was tired. He tried to close the door. The soldier shot him in the leg and left.

Bleeding heavily, Zaaf was taken to hospital. But nobody saw him until the following morning. The life of an Algerian in a French colony was no more important than that of a dog, he said. He was bandaged and sent home. Then the soldier returned to arrest him.

Zaaf was thrown without trial into the notorious Baroughia prison. He never heard what the charges were but he suspected the authorities thought he'd been smuggling, because of his frequent travel between Algeria and France. He stayed in jail for two years. Everything he owned was confiscated, including his small shop. The soldiers never found the money that he'd hidden in a locker in his room, though, and it was still there when he came back from prison. By then, prison had given him diabetes, his sight gradually went and he went to Paris for an operation he could never have had at home.

There was sympathy throughout France when the story spread. The Algerian war made many scars on the French psyche which exist even today and Zaaf received cascades of telegrams, flowers and presents. It made him feel a little better but it could never, of course, restore a life once so promising and then so brutally smashed.

Zaaf went back to Algeria and died four years later, the hero of one of the Tour's most tragicomic chapters.

A moustache, poison and blue glasses

12

The Judas Tour

Torment and pain: the suffering Raphaël Géminiani receives support from his manager Deledda.

The Judas Tour

The greatest riders have huge egos and strong wills. It couldn't be any other way to be a Tour winner. That means it's a nightmare when a team has two potential leaders. Or, as it used to be, when a national team has many stars and none of them will work together. It's been the triumph of many a manager's career to get two top names working together. For others, it's been a fiasco.

One of best examples is 1958. There were so many stars who could be in the French team. Louison Bobet, Roger Walkowiak and Jacques Anquetil had already won. And then there was Raphaël Géminiani, an electric, black-haired fighter. *Le grand fusil*, they called him, or Top Gun, if you like. His eyes could rage with anger, pop with determination or effort, fill with tears of hurt, shine with success, or smile when things sometimes went to plan. His muscular body was perfect for cycling and his only weaknesses were time-trials, where he'd lost many a stage race. Now he was in the form of his life and looking to improve on second place and best climber in 1951.

There was an odd argument that no French team could have both Géminiani and Bobet. It was odd because from 1953 to 1955 Géminiani had helped Bobet become the first man to win three consecutive Tours. It wasn't Géminiani who was the problem. The problem was Jacques Anquetil, the 1957 winner. Anquetil was ambitious and he was certain that Géminiani would ride not for him but for Bobet or for himself.

Géminiani tried to impress with several stages of strong and committed team riding in the Giro. But he wasn't picked. He went to the French manager, Marcel Bidot, to complain. He accused Anquetil of plotting to exclude him. But Bidot had seen all this before. He'd seen the time in 1953 that the French let a break get 20 minutes on a peaceful stage between the Alps and the Pyrénées because everyone felt someone else should start the chase. He wasn't going to get involved in discussing plots with Géminiani.

Anquetil had won in 1957 after stamping his authority on an unruly team. He would win the time-trials and the yellow jersey and André Darrigade would win the big sprints. Nobody else could challenge that.

But now in 1958 there was an extra threat. Géminiani didn't take his exclusion lightly. He complained so loudly that the Tour set up a whole regional team, Centre-Midi, just to support him. Fans didn't know whether to cheer the drama or cry over the bickering.

The first four days passed peacefully. Then the French national team attacked unexpectedly early in the fifth. Bobet and Anquetil took off in a small group with the ever-vigilant Géminiani. Only Planckaert and Nencini of the other favourites were with them. The others, especially Gaul and Brankaert, were dozing. A crash at the front of the bunch made a chase impossible and the break approached the finish with two minutes' lead.

Now, Géminiani was no sprinter. There was a minute's bonus for the winner and he didn't want a favourite to get it and win the yellow jersey. He therefore offered a lead-out to Sabbadini, a sprinter from another regional team. Anquetil and Bobet appealed to Sabbadini's patriotism. To which Géminiani said: 'To hell with them! Keep yourself two wheel-lengths ahead at the finish. That's all I ask of you.'

Sabbadini managed it, took the stage and a minute's bonus, and a lesser-known rider called Bauvin became the *maillot jaune*.

Still the French nationals didn't see Géminiani as the great threat. But destiny had decided that a seemingly quiet stage next day from Caen to St-Brieuc would be his great triumph.

It looked at first like a great French victory. Four of the national team got into a break so fast that they were going to share the yellow, green, mountain and team competitions between them. Bidot cheered. In the peloton, Anquetil and Bobet relaxed and let the other teams do the work. They were confident enough to drift to the back of the field without a care.

It was then that Géminiani rode alongside Nencini, the Italian leader, and discreetly pointed them out.

'If you were to attack,' he suggested, 'I wouldn't bother you. I'd rather see you win than them.'

The Italian understood immediately. He got together a breakaway with Adriaenssens, Anglade, Planckaert and others –

and yet still the French dawdled in their triumph. It was Radio Tour that woke Bidot. Eventually he got a message to Anquetil and Bobet. Now they had to organise and do the chasing themselves. They turned to Géminiani but got nothing but mockery.

'What do you say? Who is this Nencini? He's of no interest to me, and anyway I didn't see a thing.'

They begged him to join the chase.

'There must be something wrong with your eyesight,' he chided. 'Haven't you seen the colour of my jersey? Not the same as yours so far as I can see. No, you'll have to do your own legwork.'

And so they had to. Bidot told the four in the break to stop working. Nencini's chasers caught them and Bidot's quartet then worked on slowing down the whole lot. The glory of France had vanished in a very short time and Bidot was furious.

Symbolically there was a storm breaking. Géminiani took it as a sign and threw himself into a furious attack with 25km to go. Only Mahé of the French team followed. Géminiani gave it everything and they got 10 minutes. It put Géminiani in third place and as he came to a standstill and swung his leg over the leather saddle, he said: 'It is as I have always said: I will win the Tour.'

The French feared mainly Charly Gaul of Luxembourg, the Angel of the Mountains. He could switch into an impossibly low gear and tear apart any field and its plans. His trouble was that he was unpopular. He had a childish side. As a 22-year-old making his debut in the 1955 team he'd refused to share his money. His team-mates refused to protect him and he came third. He should have won and it taught him to share. But pelotons have long memories.

Gaul created a sensation two days after the Nencini debacle by winning the first lone time-trial – in front of Anquetil. There was no greater specialist than Maître Jacques and the man who cruised on high gears had now been belittled by a man who twiddled tiny ones.

Géminiani overcame his weakness and came sixth. The French journalist Francis Huger wrote, remarking on Géminiani's conk:

'Géminiani's nose! It contains all his senses. With that he feels, sees, hears, smells and tastes. Maybe he even pushes his pedals with this phenomenal nose. I have yet to work that out, but he is definitely number three in the overall standings.'

Now he was on a crusade. He was the best-placed favourite at the foot of the Pyrénées and 10 minutes up on Gaul.

'Who will be holding Gaul's back wheel over the peaks?' he teased reporters. 'Look carefully and see if it isn't me.' And so it was, over the Aubisque and then to the finish. Géminiani was wearing yellow for the first time in nine Tours.

'A new career begins,' wrote *L'Equipe* about this 33-year-old. He had always been loyal to Bobet and now he was writing a new chapter with himself as its hero. But all the same, Géminiani grew nervous. He ate in his room instead of with his team. He became quiet and introverted even though his team was enthusiastic and riding well. He had realised that there is a great difference between attacking and being attacked.

Twenty times Gaul attacked on the second great Alpine stage. And 20 times Géminiani repelled him. But then a group got away on the descent of the Peyresourde and the Italian Favero took Géminiani's yellow jersey with the bonus he got for finishing second.

The tough time-trial up Mont Ventoux had been feared for many years by everyone except the climbers. Géminiani retrieved his *maillot jaune*.

'This is my answer to Gaul', he chirruped, cheered by the arrival of his father. 'I will attack tomorrow. I want revenge.'

The stage went to Gap in the French highlands. Géminiani took off. Gaul had mechanical problems, lost eight minutes and, seemingly, the Tour. The leaders reached the final peak and Géminiani turned a blind eye when Nencini attacked Anquetil. The French team-leader berated him for letting it happen.

Géminiani sneered.

'You ride your Tour and I'll ride mine,' he snapped.

It wasn't a wise remark. You need friends at this stage of the race when you're in yellow. Géminiani should have tried reconciliation. He'd lost several team-mates from the rough going and now support from the French national team could have saved his victory. But that wasn't Géminiani's way. He believed he could do everything with the help of just his few team-mates at Centre-Midi.

And to be fair, for a while he could. Things went well on the hard stage from Gap to Briançon, where so many others had perished over the years, and now there remained just Briançon – Aix-les-Bains and its four great peaks. It was here that hell awaited.

The weather gods promised snow for openers and then a mixture of slush, hail and more snow on the passes. It was perfect for Gaul. He grew happier as the weather worsened. Come the sun and he could be the first to quit, but black clouds and sweeping rain were his delight.

Gaul spread his wings and flew. Géminiani's legs were bad but he was obsessed by not losing a metre to Anquetil. He lost contact on the first climb, then found him again. Favero, whom the French were finally taking seriously, attacked just as Géminiani broke his toe clip. He should have pressed on but Géminiani saw himself already as the great suffering hero and insisted on changing pedals. The result was to lose contact with the others. And his common-sense as well.

He became obsessed. Others pushed newspapers under their jerseys to stem the mountain cold; Géminiani rode down the mountains regardless. Others grabbed their *musettes* of food; Géminiani ignored them. And he paid the price. Exhaustion gripped him like a vice. He lost 15 minutes to Gaul and limped on pitifully with the loyal Dotto helping him. Things went still worse for Anquetil. He lost more than 23 minutes and left the race next day with a lung infection.

Pictures of the exhausted Géminiani filled the papers. They showed him being grabbed by Deledda, his manager, to stop his tumbling from tiredness at the finish. He lost but the French saw echoes of the old stars who rode hundreds of kilometres through the night on roads like cow tracks.

Michel Clare said in *L'Equipe*: 'He still wore the yellow jersey, but large tears poured from his eyes. A suppressed shudder filled his chest. Of all the sporting dramas that I have followed, none has been so heartrending. I don't believe that anyone who was a witness to this theatre of Hades could avoid their hearts being flayed or their souls being filled with compassion.

'What could one do? Or say? It would be necessary to create a new language to still the storm that the loss on this tragic day created. Nothing could replace the shattered dream and I am sure that, until the end of his days, he will constantly return to the grey pictures from this Wednesday in July.

'He shook from cold, from exhaustion, from the pain of everything. He had aged ten years. His eyes were expressionless, his jaw moved involuntarily from cramps. They threw a windproof raincoat over him. He cowered under it so that his back became hunched. He allowed himself to be led to a car, so that he could be driven back to his hotel where the only comfort was waiting for him: the friendship of his team-mates.'

But Top Gun wasn't quite as broken as he seemed through the eyes of pity. Through tears he delivered this tirade in a weak voice, several times giving in to quiet sobbing:

'It was too hard. I could do no more. They all wanted me dead. They all attacked me. It was no longer possible. I broke down. The whole French team was against me. They are Judases, every one of them!'

What theatre! They understand tragedy, the French, whether they're on the stage or merely watching. Is it surprising the whole world was taken in?

You ought to know that Géminiani got back in the saddle again. He came third overall. Two days after Géminiani's day in the mountains, Gaul won the final time trial, the yellow jersey and his only Tour de France.

Géminiani's career ended when he too caught malaria on the African trip that cost Fausto Coppi his life. But he survived and with delicious irony he went on to become a manager for, among others, Jacques Anquetil.

A moustache, poison and blue glasses

13

Summer training for the winter

Parc des Princes velodrome: In 1958 one of the most spectacular but ultimately tragic events in Tour history when 50 metres from the line an official collided with André Darrigade. The 70 year old official later died from the impact.

Summer training for the winter

The whole world has heard of Hans Christian Andersen. Denmark's teller of fairy tales is as famous as the little mermaid in Copenhagen harbour. But hands up who has heard of Hans E. Andresen.

You don't know? Well, Hans E. Andresen was the first Danish cyclist to finish the Tour de France, and in 1958 he had a front-row seat for the drama between Gaul, Anquetil, Bobet and Géminiani.

Four Danes were part of an international team whose stars were the Austrian Christian, who'd come third the year before, Shay Elliott from Ireland, and Stan Brittain and Brian Robinson from Britain. The Danes quickly felt the heat. A puncture eliminated Fritz Ravn on the first stage; Eluf Dalgaard got as far as the seventh; and Kaj Allan Olsen was eliminated on time at the tenth. Andresen was the only Dane left and he put up a brave fight.

The Danish papers wrote more and more about him as it became clear he was determined to finish. There were occasions when the time limit threatened to halt him but he escaped every time. It could be close: he once had to attack two other tailenders when he realised how parlous their situation was; he scraped in but the other two were thrown out for the sake of 20 seconds.

The Danish papers didn't see the broader picture. The Tour was Hans E. Andresen.

'Hans E... the man of the day in today's Tour de France,' they wrote. 'Little Hans E had problems with the heat but gritted his teeth. The sweat poured from his brow during the two climbs on the stage. He stood straight up in the saddle and pushed his pedals so that you could hear the metal groan. The spectators at the finish could hardly believe their eyes when they saw the Dane cross the line in fifth place with the same time as the winner of the stage. Hans E. Andresen was the undisputed champion of the day. The lowlander had done what no one thought possible: he had escorted the big guns home...'

Ah well, the odd Frenchmen or two might have noticed in passing that André Darrigade had won the stage.

On the stage through hell in the Judas Tour, 'Denmark's Hans E', as he was now known in all the papers, surprised many by finishing 33rd.

And then he reached Paris.

'Denmark's only remaining competitor, the little, tough, red-haired Hans E. Andresen, also survived the final stage and rode a lap of honour around the stadium with other cyclists from the International team – the Portuguese Barbosa, the Austrian Christian and the Irishman Elliott. The enthusiastic Frenchmen, who had followed the race's daily bulletins with great excitement, rose from their seats and acclaimed the riders – not least Hans E – for their effort.'

The Danish Cycling Union held a reception for Andresen when he got home. There were several gifts, including a fishing rod from the Lyngby cycling club. Being a professional certainly had its advantages; he'd never have been able to accept such wonderful things if he'd still been an amateur.

There was a 'Tour revenge' meeting on the Ordrup track next day with members of the International team. Eight thousand cheered the first Danish Tour hero, who responded by winning everything. He told a reporter: 'I wanted to get to Paris even if meant walking the last stretch barefooted.'

Andresen was my hero too, that summer. He'd already won silver at the amateur world championship, won a stage race in Egypt and come second in the Peace Race. The Danes could follow the Peace Race on East German radio; the problem was having to listen to the production figures of every village that it passed through.

Let's move now to March 1996. Nearly 40 years have passed and I had to know how he felt.

'Hans, someone wants to talk to you about the Tour de France,' I heard Mrs Andresen call.

(In the background: 'Of course. It's like that every year at this time.')

Now Hans E himself.

'Sure, it was OK, but I didn't consider it all that important' he said. 'I was using it as summer training for the winter track season. It was my final year as a rider and the real money was in the six-day races, so it meant getting into shape. I could do that with the Tour de France, where all my expenses were paid.

Otherwise there was no real money there.

'We got £7 a day but the organisers sent home our miracle masseur, Piet van der Heyde, when all the other Danes retired. He knew the race inside out and he could have given us some good advice. I had to pay my mechanic, Henry Pedersen myself. He stayed and helped me through the rest of the race. Had I not paid him he would have been forced to return home as well.

'Jorgen Beyerholm (a Danish journalist and enthusiast), who had arranged the contract for the race, rang some time afterwards to say that I was due £120 in prize money – but it had already been allocated.

'There'd been no real cohesion in the International team, but that was really not my fault. Elliott, Robinson and Christian wouldn't share the prize money with anyone but me, because they knew me from previous races. They didn't believe in the other Danes, and I'd have none of that so we all rode for ourselves.

'Henry Pedersen had a temporary place in a service car but he couldn't see everything, so I rode with a spare tyre round my neck in case I had a puncture. We didn't have extra equipment like the others, either.

'I don't really think about it very often. I'll always have regrets. Regrets about lost possibilities and opportunities that I wish I'd taken. Besides there are other things in my career that I feel were greater, not least the world championship silver.

'And that stage to Aix? That was really hard, with the snow. But Gaul, he was fantastic. A thin little guy. His legs were no bigger than my arms but there was certainly nothing wrong with his heart or his lungs. And Anquetil impressed me when he got off his bike, coughed up phlegm full of blood and then got back on his bike and rode on.

'And Darrigade was a tough old dog. He fell 30km from the finish in Paris, bounced along the road and scraped all his fingers until they bled. He got an injection to prevent cramping and kept on riding. Suddenly he was alone and 200 metres in front of the field. He'd beaten his injury but in the stadium an observer wandered too far on to the track and it was a very sad end for Darrigade, who had to go to hospital. In spite of not completing the race, he still came high on the final result list. That was only right.

'My press cuttings are all in two large sacks in the loft. This past winter we finally got them down and started – mostly Birgit – to put them in some kind of order so that my grandchildren can see what I was up to then.

'In 1959 I didn't ride. There is something called family, and after all I was almost finished with cycling.'

Like Britain, it took a long time for Denmark to establish itself on the cycling map. And just as Britain has had world champions and yellow jerseys since the days of Robinson and Brittain, so Denmark too has made a name for itself in the Tour de France.

By the way, we northern Europeans sometimes look at the more excitable French journalists and wonder if they can bear to read their stories again in the cold of next morning. Well, I'm afraid the same can be said of my fellow Danish journalists and their glorification of their lone countryman in 1958.

And another confession. For years I always thought that Hans was the first Dane to ride. Now I find there was a Christian Christensen in the Tour of 1913. Andresen is still the first Dane to finish officially, though. Poor Christensen took a wrong turn on the unlucky 13th stage, took several hours to get back to the right route and arrived at the finish so late the judges had had enough and left him off the results.

He carried on riding as an individual and got to Paris, even if he was not classified in the official rankings.

A moustache, poison and blue glasses

14

The life of Brian

National hero:
In 1958 Brian
Robinson became
the first British rider
to win a stage of
the Tour de France.
A member of the
British team that
rode in the 1955
Tour, he was a fine
rider and achieved
success on the
Continent before
Tom Simpson,
Barry Hoban and
Robert Millar.

The life of Brian

Brian Robinson was overjoyed when the little service car came up behind him. It meant he had put Jean Dotto so far behind him that his breakaway was no longer in doubt. A moment later he heard that he had two and a half minutes. It was up to him now to fulfil the plan he'd had since he learned the Tour route for 1959.

Many thoughts ran through his mind. If only the peloton would be kind enough not to chase. He felt the odds favoured him even if it was a stage of no less than 202km.

The previous day had been the last with major difficulties in the mountains. The next day would be the last big time-trial, the last chance for the leading riders to challenge each other. That meant the generals would want a rest day, and anyway Robinson had been no threat to them since a disastrous 13th stage.

Until then he'd been in the top ten. But then he had a day so bad that he fought to get to the finish within the time limit. He didn't make it, but the Tour let him start again next day as a reward for the way he'd ridden so far. His team-mate, Shay Elliott, had stayed behind with him but he hadn't been shown the same pardon. He'd had to leave the race. Now Robinson felt he had to do something to justify his friend's solidarity, like winning a stage.

His legs went on auto-pilot and he smiled. A good steady rhythm let him pull further ahead of the bunch minute by minute. He remembered the triumphant day the year before when he became the first British rider to win a stage. It was the eighth day, from St-Brieve to Brest. Galdeano had been away early and Robinson had seized the chance himself when the Spaniard was caught after 50km. Dotto joined him a few kilometres later and then the Italian Padovan. A chase had set up but the trio held two minutes and then pulled ahead to five.

Twelve kilometres from the finish Robinson had tried to leave the other two but Dotto proved undroppable, coming back from however far back Robinson left him, and Padovan refused to shift from the Englishman's wheel.

That meant a sprint finish. Dotto stood no chance and left it to the other two. They raced for the line, Robinson trying to pass on the right but Padovan swinging over to block him. Then Robinson went to the left, and again Padovan moved over to halt him. The judges saw it all and they downgraded him to second. Robinson had won first prize and an award as the most aggressive rider. What a day!

Robinson smiled again in his nostalgia. He'd never imagined how many people could want to interview him in a single day. And it made for good appearance contracts after the Tour, too.

This called for a repetition. His eyes fell on stage 20 when the Tour route for 1959 was published. It went through almost English landscape, with many minor hills and undulations. Robinson knew it would be like his home in Yorkshire. He talked it over with his team manager, Ducazeaux, the best he'd had. The Frenchman, who ran a restaurant in Paris with his wife when he wasn't racing, could teach even an experienced rider a lot. He'd guided Louison Bobet to a win in the Giro in 1958 and he knew how to encourage a man, how to build him for a special occasion, how to concentrate on a goal and believe in success.

Robinson prepared with new light Italian wheels with just 28 spokes. He used 8oz tyres he'd intended for the time-trial.

The stage left Annecy and he felt good. Gerard Saint, normally his team-mate, was riding in the Tour for a French regional team and was second in the mountains competition. Saint quietly asked Robinson to help him over the only difficulty of the stage, the col d'Challon, and the final piece of the puzzle fell into place. He could now draw his friend to the top, camouflaging his own intentions, and shoot off as soon as Saint had won the climb.

It went just as he planned. He started a furious descent, making the most of a natural ability. Dotto tried to catch up but disappeared, although Robinson didn't dare look round to be sure. He concentrated on the best line to spare his thin tyres and begged that they wouldn't puncture.

Now the service car was behind him, which the officials would never have allowed until he was far enough ahead for the driver not to interfere with the race. The field was just waiting for him to collapse. There were more than 130km to go. Suddenly he felt happier with that 13th stage. After all, the bunch would never have allowed him this liberty if he hadn't lost so much time then. Every kilometre boosted his morale. His pulse was pounding and every heartbeat stamped out 'I'm going to win... this is the day... this is for Shay.'

He was three minutes ahead at 82km and seven minutes 23km later. He reckoned that 10 minutes by the town of St-Amour would be all he needed. Then there'd be 60km to the finish. He got there to find he had an incredible 17 minutes. Now he was euphoric.

'My legs were good, my confidence formidable. I was fully psyched up and feeling 110 per cent. I started to think of all the contracts that were waiting for me after the Tour now that I was certain that a win was in the bag. Even if I was primarily proud of the athletic effort, the money is always agreeable,' he reflects now.

Just one scare remained. The head wind was strong and the stage route map seemed to imply that the last 40km were on flat, exposed roads. But they weren't. They went through woods and there was no danger.

He didn't celebrate a second too early. He concentrated on every metre until he passed the line in Chalon-sur-Saône. He had no less than 20:06 minutes to wait before Padovan won the sprint ahead of Darrigade. And during those 20 minutes nothing could divert attention from the English hero.

'It's difficult to describe the feelings of satisfaction, stimulation, pleasure, excitement... all these things and, of course, the public appreciation, are so overwhelming that it brings tears of joy. Also the family and the friends at home share in the triumph to such a degree that even today it stirs the blood when someone reminds me of those super moments.'

Brian Robinson didn't enter just British cycling history. I phoned *L'Equipe* to get some facts about the stage and I only had to say the name for journalist Philip Sudre to start quoting facts: 'Brian Robinson: two stage wins, Brest 1958, Chalon-sur-Saône 1959, in Chalon after a solo ride of around 150km. The first *anglais* to win a stage, a formidable rider, a...' and so it went on.

Quite something in the life of Brian.

15

The spirit of '64

Lap of honour: Poulidor (left) and Anquetil at the Parc des Prince velodrome in 1964. A sauve sophisticated rider and stage race specialist, *Maître Jacques* won the Tour five times.

The spirit of '64

Have you ever been so sure that you've been somewhere that you can recount what it was like, what you saw, what happened? I have. The 1964 Tour de France is like that for me. It's so real for me that people ask me to show them pictures, give them a slide show and a talk. And then I realise that, no, I wasn't there. The only pictures are in my head. But there are so many dramatic images and I've seen them so many times that I feel I was there.

Let me give you the slide show anyway.

Ladies and gentlemen...

In my country, in Denmark, we have always loved the glorious and marginal defeats that have managed to make our country even smaller. The expression 'spirit of '64' relates to 1864 and the heroism of the Danish soldiers as they were crushed by the Prussians.

In France, though, it means something completely different. There they talk not of 1864 but of 1964 and the most fantastic Tour de France of all. This was the Tour of spirit. It was the experience of my life. It was a privilege to be there, to follow each stage, and to take these pictures.

I'll start at the end. On this first picture you see two riders on their lap of honour in Paris. On the left is Raymond Poulidor. He's bursting with health after more than 4,000km round France. He's smiling to the spectators who are cheering him and he has his arm protectively round his companion's shoulder.

On the right we see Jacques Anquetil. Look at the hollow cheeks, the eyes burning from deep cavities, his whole demeanour completely worn. What has he been through? How much has he suffered? Anquetil and Poulidor both have the laurels and the trappings of acclaim. If you don't already know, see if you can guess which of them won the Tour. I'll come back to it at the end.

The next picture is the start of the race, in the market place in Rennes in central Brittany. You see the same people. Poulidor, the much-loved Pou-Pou, is once again ready to challenge Maître Jacques. And *maître* in French means not the name we call a small boy but the respect given to an expert, a master of his craft. That's not surprising. Anquetil has already won the Tour four times. He's one of the greatest cyclists in history.

Poulidor, on the other hand, is the man of the people. He's charming, an excellent mountain rider, but he's missing some vital qualities. He's not as strong or as calculating as Anquetil. Anquetil has the race planned; he knows where to attack, where to get his time bonuses, where to send his team-mates in a break so that Poulidor doesn't get a bonus.

The drama starts on the first stage. There's a crash three kilometres from the finish. Rik Van Looy goes down, one of the men who could threaten the French favourites. He's concussed but he gets back on to his bike and finishes this stage and the next, but then it's over.

I can't resist showing you this picture from 1962. It's Van Looy again and it'll show you how unlucky he could be. A motorbike rode past the field and it threw up a stone into van Looy's kidneys. Get hit there and it's very painful. That, after all, is why boxing coaches talk of 'getting a crafty blow in the kidneys.' It would take out any fighter. And it took Van Looy out. He didn't get to the finish.

Anyway, to get back to 1964...

Normally the first days of the Tour are peaceful. The huge pack of journalists had the usual 24 hours of hard work but in 1964 they could have used an extra 12 hours a day to describe the drama they were to experience. In this picture we see André Darrigade winning his 21st stage, on the second day in Amiens. He's dreaming of beating the record of 25 but he's already 37 and he's got to hurry. The Tour was always his in the days before the mountains. He won the first stage for five years running but it was usually over for him when the mountains came.

Here we see the end of the fifth stage from Metz to Freiburt. The Tour has many times had political undertones in Alsace-Lorraine, but now the Germany economic interests were so big that it was time to take the Tour deeper into the real Germany. It was such a success that next year the Tour started in Cologne.

The Germans have a top name in Rudi Altig, a tall man with a crew-cut who had won a furious sprint with the Dutchmen Janssen and Nijdam to take the green points jersey. He's also ridden into a position that could bring him a stage win and yellow jersey on German soil.

In this picture, though, Altig is in second place. He's defended one attack after another from the first kilometre and now he's showing that this stage is his and his alone even though he's Anquetil's team-mate. He takes off with Georges Groussard. Three others join them and they're never in danger of being caught.

Four of the five work hard together. The fifth, the Belgian Willy Derboven, is sitting in to protect his team-mate van de Kerckhove, who's got the yellow jersey. That annoys the Germans. Altig can take the *maillot jaune* if the break stays away but in those days it was still unethical to sit in and win the stage. Which is just what Derboven's doing.

Anquetil, as you can see in this next picture, is furious with Altig. He isn't worried that he'd taken the yellow jersey but he is angry that he'd taken Groussard with him. He's telling Altig that Groussard is strong in the mountains and now Altig has taken him well ahead of Anquetil.

Anquetil was right. He saw things very clearly. He wasn't at his fittest. He'd won the Giro d'Italia 14 days earlier and he hadn't recovered from the hard time the Italians had given him. Groussard took the yellow jersey on the eighth stage, the first in the mountains. Anquetil had reason not to thank Altig.

This picture shows Federico Bahamontes, who won that stage. It made him second overall behind Groussard. With a bit more intelligent riding he could have won more than one Tour de France. But then again perhaps he was only interested in being the king of the mountains. He was 35 but he could still climb like a goat and kick away all the attacks on the climb of the Galibier.

Raymond Poulidor finished second to Bahamontes that day, collected 30 seconds' bonus and moved into third place. Anquetil was eighth, almost a minute behind him.

Arch rivals: Jacques Anquteil (left) and Raymond Poulidor battle for the best line. Poulidor rode the Tour fourteen times, from 1962 to 1976 coming second three times but never winning. He was therefore known as "the eternal second!"

You can think of Bahamontes and Groussard now as only bit-players. They soon leave the spotlight. The real stars of the drama are Anquetil and Poulidor.

They are to France as Coppi and Bartali had been a decade earlier to Italy. The intellectuals follow Anquetil; the romantics are behind Poulidor. Right now they're working out their prospects. They're thinking of the time bonuses to the stage winner on the descent from the col de Restefond on the second mountain stage. The finish is in the vélodrome at Monte Carlo.

Poulidor is first past the line in this picture. He raises his arm in victory but Anquetil and everyone else realise there's still another lap to go. Anquetil starts a long dash for the line and with it the minute's bonus that was Poulidor's worst dream.

Look at Poulidor in this picture, hurling his bike to the ground in anger and disgust! But who's to blame? Poulidor, I'm afraid. He hadn't read his stage description properly.

The next day we see Anquetil in his perfect style in the time-trial. It was rare he was ever beaten here. Some of his Tour wins had come from individual time-trials and on this day he advanced to second behind Groussard, who was as devoted to defending his yellow jersey as Anquetil had feared.

And now finally some peaceful days. The best stories were about the heat, which you can almost feel from this picture of the field rolling along between the Alps and the Pyrénées. One problem was that the tar began to melt. It was like riding in porridge. And another problem was sleeping at night. Most hotels in those days didn't have air conditioning and the temperature didn't drop below 20.

Only the Spaniard, Julio Jimenez, dared to break away and here you see him putting eight minutes between himself and the rest of the field.

Here in this photograph we can see just how satisfied Anquetil is. So satisfied, perhaps, that he behaves unprofessionally for the first time in his Tour career. He eats and drinks in the sun on the rest day in Andorra. The journalists can't believe it. Here is the usually terse cycling general joking and drinking champagne between bites of grilled meat.

That was paradise. Nemesis followed next day. The stage moved straight up towards the col d'Envalira. The weather had changed. Clouds hid the mountain and the field rode in light rain. Anquetil was clearly in big trouble, close to giving up. We can see him here with his team-mate Louis Rostollan beside him. The team manager has told Rostollan to work on Anquetil's morale and get him through the day.

'Have you forgotten your name is Anquetil?' he's chiding him. 'Me, I can abandon without it bothering anyone but a few friends. But you are Anquetil. You have millions of fans. It's your duty to grit your teeth and continue. Do you really want to give the Tour to Poulidor?'

There's no answer. Anquetil's eyes are glazed. He gets out of the saddle and carries on riding that way, as though getting back into the saddle would cost him energy he badly needs. Rostollan makes sure Anquetil gets enough to drink, pushes and pulls him up the mountain. But it costs them four minutes on the others.

This next picture could have been taken anywhere. It shows the team cars and the spare bikes from behind. They're on their way down a mountain in fog and rain. I've included it because it was the rear lights that Anquetil used as his descent beacons, just like an aircraft landing. He could read the route from the brake lights that picked out every hairpin. He could ride blind and make up time, living on his reflexes. He took horrible chances. And slowly his body began to recover. He had to win, he had to have a record five Tours.

He was halfway to Poulidor before he reached the valley, and then he caught the group that included Groussard and his teammates. Groussard rode for Pelforth and Anquetil for another drinks company, St Raphaël. Normally it would make them enemies. But here Groussard was riding for his yellow jersey and for once it made them allies. After a while they catch the leaders.

And then... unbelievable! On the day when Anquetil is close to abandoning, Poulidor has a puncture. His car is there immediately with a new bike but the mechanic is so nervous that he throws the bike from the car, it hits Poulidor, he falls and the chain comes off.

Suddenly it's Poulidor who's lagging, and in Toulouse he's 2:34 behind Anquetil. He's furious the next day and he puts a minute between himself and the field on the way from Toulouse to Luchon, but Anquetil stays calm. His philosophy is that you pay for that kind of luxury in the days that follow.

And here's Federico Bahamontes again, the eagle of Toledo. This time he's the winner of the classic Pyrénées stage over the four peaks: Peyresourde, Aspin, Tourmalet and Aubisque. It was his last chance to win the 1964 Tour but he had to take the yellow jersey that day. He wouldn't do it, though. He was 36 seconds short – one for each year of his age next day. It was too much but he could still be king of the mountains for the sixth and – as it would turn out – last time.

Scenes of delight in Bordeaux. The people there claimed Darrigade as their own – not entirely accurately, because he actually lived nearby in Dax. They'd been waiting a long time to see him win in Bordeaux. Now he'd manage Bordeaux's dream by producing win number 22 there. No winner in Paris ever got greater adulation. And he'd managed it only just in time. Never again would he win a stage of the Tour de France. And never would he beat André Leducq's 25 stage wins. Eddy Merckx won 34 and Bernard Hinault 28, but the fair-haired, balding figure of Darrigade had to settle for 22.

But how quickly jubilation can turn to sorrow. This is the picture next day. You can see the horrific scenes just after a heavy police vehicle has driven into a group of spectators in Port de Couze, gone on through the railings of a bridge and then fallen into a canal. Eight people died and there were long discussions about the efficiency of the rescue operation. I certainly hope I never need help in the middle of a Tour de France stage; in some places the traffic comes to a standstill 40km from the race.

Fortunately this next photo is of a sporting nature. It shows the culmination of the duel between Anquetil and Poulidor. It's the final challenge in the mountains. The date is July 12 and we're on the Puy-de-Dôme, the highest peak in the Auvergne. Jimenez takes off. Bahamontes follows him. Anquetil is on Poulidor's wheel and he's starting to tire. He needs a bluff.

From behind Poulidor's back he curses: 'Damn... the Spaniards will get the bonuses!'

Poulidor falls for it.

'Anquetil must have good legs if he's already thinking of the finish bonuses,' he thinks. 'I can't let the Spaniards go. How long can I wait? I've got to break Anquetil, but when, and how?'

He hesitates before going after Bahamontes. Anquetil moves up alongside. He'll have Poulidor under control if he can stay there. Even so, there's a washboard of furrows on his forehead and his face is blank. This is a man riding on will alone. Blow and he'll fall. But Poulidor daren't blow.

Spectators are breathless with excitement. One of them must fold. But which?

The red triangle of the final kilometre spans the road. Anquetil falls a little behind. Poulidor sees it and drives on. In a second he's gone. He takes 42 seconds in the last 800m, but it's too few. The yellow jersey hangs from a 14-second thread with only two days to go.

Anquetil makes no mistakes on the last but one day. The 311km are on flat main roads. Next day is a split stage. Nothing happens in the morning, into Versailles, so the whole Tour de France depends on the last 27.5km, a time-trial from Versailles to the Parc des Princes.

This picture shows how everyone is ready for the final act. It's July 14, Bastille Day, the biggest French holiday. Nine out of ten Frenchmen want Pou-Pou to take little more than a second per kilometre, to dethrone the King.

The race starts in reverse order to the overall result. Anquetil is last to leave, Poulidor immediately ahead. *Cinq... quatre... trois...* Poulidor starts. Crowds line the route and they produce a whirlwind of cheers and encouragement. Then Anquetil. He is whistled, with just a few cheers in the background.

Eight hundred thousand are by the roadside. The rest of France is watching television or listening to the radio. Commentators stand at every kilometre. The difference between the two men is broadcast constantly. Anquetil is favourite, but the yellow jersey can be surprisingly heavy. And what if one of them punctured, like Poulidor in that first time-trial? He'd lost 14 seconds then. Think how many times he could have found a paltry 14 seconds in 4,500 kilometres.

Halfway. Only six seconds in Anquetil's favour. But not for nothing is he the king of the time-trial. He racks into his highest gear and flails it mercilessly. He wins by 21 seconds. He gets 20 seconds as a bonus and Poulidor gets nothing. Altig comes second and Anquetil wins the Tour of 1964 by 55 seconds.

And here we are back at the first photo. Did you guess the winner? It's the hollow-cheeked, exhausted, starved but very determined psychological genius of a wreck on the right. Once again he'd beaten Poulidor and now he'd won a record five Tours. Poulidor never did win but next year and as late as 1974 he finished second.

Whisper 'the spirit of '64' to any French cycling fan. He'll know what you mean.

16

A cannibal
in the shadow

The Cannibal: Riding the Tour for the first time in 1969, Eddy Merckx dominated the peloton, beating his great rival Felix Gimondi by more than 16 minutes. The greatest Tour rider in history!

A cannibal in the shadow

The Tour de France waited with longing for Eddy Merckx. So many years had passed since a Belgian had won – one had to go back to Sylvere Maes in 1939 in fact. And a wait like that hurts a true bike-loving nation.

Merckx was exceptional. He turned professional in 1965, won nine races in his first year and 20 in his second, including Milan-San Remo. He was clearly going to be one of the greats, a natural for the Tour. So what the hell was he waiting for?

It was the question he asked when he met his adviser, his employer and his team manager in January 1967. The French watched him defend his Milan-San Remo and felt sure he'd ride. But instead, he tackled 'just' the Giro d'Italia.

It gave him two great victories, one of them a difficult mountain stage. He finished ninth, with vital experience of how to ride a three-week stage race, about mountain riding, and about the toughness you need when you fall ill. In his case it was flu, a 39-degree fever that stopped him fighting for victory.

Later that year he became world champion, and in 1968 he won Paris-Roubaix, the 'Sunday in Hell'. Now he simply *had* to ride the Tour. But no. His respect for it was too great. He'd do it only when he was ready, not like Federico Bahamontes.

Bahamontes made his debut in 1954 and found the only thing he could do well was climb. That was the year he outpaced the field on the col de Peyresourde, got off his bike at the top, ate an ice cream, had a drink from a stream and then rode on as the first few passed. It made him hugely popular with his fans but in coming years he realised just how disrespectful he'd been to the Tour de France, no less.

Belgium wasn't prepared to wait for Merckx to get still further experience from the Giro. '*Eddy naar de Ronde!*' it chorused – Merckx must ride the Tour. Even the prime minister became involved, inviting Merckx and other cycling figures to a pow-wow over lunch.

Merckx wrote in his biography that the prime minister told him: 'You should not let yourself become influenced by the pressure you are getting, and will continue to be put under, in connection with the Tour de France. You should be sensible and not get into something that you do not feel is in your best interest. I am as other Belgians: I hope that you take part in this Tour because you are the one with the best chance of taking the yellow jersey. But you are at liberty to make your own choice.'

It was incredible that Merckx could stay away from the Tour for so long, but at least it shows that employers and managers know and have respect for their sport. Merckx believed Peugeot would have destroyed his career if it had used him in 1966 or 1967, even if he'd done a good job. Of influence, no doubt, was the fact that his personal manager and adviser, Jean van Buggenhout, followed him when he changed teams. Despite the pressure, Merckx rode only the Giro in 1968, and won it easily.

So 1969 was the year. Now the Giro was only preparation, not a target. He was leading by a huge margin after 19 stages when the bomb dropped.

'Merckx positive for drugs' said the newspaper headlines. He was disqualified.

It was an absurd situation. He'd been tested eight times, each time with a negative result. He protested. It was a mistake. Or sabotage perhaps. Did someone want to present the victory to Felice Gimondi? Or perhaps there was a plot to stop his taking part in the Tour.

He gave further urine samples to his team manager in the presence of journalists from Belgium, France and Italy. They went express to Milan, were tested and were cleared of anything criminal. He was banned for a month nevertheless, just long enough to stop his starting in the Tour. Belgium appealed and the international body, the UCI, suspended the sentence. But it didn't clear him.

Merckx was furious. Stuck at home, he even considered throwing in cycling. He'd won almost everything except the Tour, he wasn't short of money. Why carry on?

Belgium is a small country and it produces few champions. But it did have a Formula One star in Jacky Ickx, and it was Ickx who broke through his isolation. He talked to him about what was missing in his career, talked to him about Belgium. Merckx relented. 'I'm not a chauvinist,' he said, 'but I love my country.'

So he started in the Tour and took out his anger on the roads of France. And it was there that he realised his reputation had travelled. He and his team were pitched against the whole race. If there was a break, they waited for him to bring it back. There would be no help.

He attacked on the seventh day, when the finish was at the peak of the Ballon d'Alsace. He whipped his team to a hard tempo to the foot and then took control. One by one the others lost touch. The last survivor was Rudi Altig. Merckx got to the finish alone, took the yellow jersey and let nobody take it back.

The previous year a former team-mate, Christian Raymond, had nicknamed him the Cannibal because he consumed everyone, won everything. Now he lived up to the name. Merckx won the yellow jersey, the green points jersey and the mountain competition. He held the white jersey as best placed in the other three.

And yet he began to be boring. Now everybody else raced for second place, not to beat Merckx, which many riders didn't think possible or at least worth the effort. It was hugely unfair. It wasn't Merckx's fault he was so much better. It hurt him and it provoked one of the greatest efforts of the Tour.

It started on the Tourmalet. He sprinted over it to ensure his climbing competition, sped down the other side in the safety of being alone, then noted he had a secure lead at the bottom. Then it struck him that he didn't have to wait for the others. He switched on the turbo and pushed himself so much in the last 20km that he admitted he almost blacked out.

'My tongue felt like a rake,' he recalled, 'swollen like a rotting fish. And my teeth were ground together. But I was glad I had that day.'

The cycling world surrendered itself to him. 'Cannibal' was a name of honour for the first time. Belgium was happier than on liberation day. There were Eddy Merckx tea-towels, Eddy Merckx chewing gum, key-rings and T-shirts. There were even posters of Eddy Merckx's bare backside, taken in a changing room by an opportunist snapshotter and quickly banned by court order.

There were Merckx jokes:

'Why were Merckx, Poulidor and Gimondi fined on the Tourmalet?'

'Poulidor and Gimondi for letting themselves be pulled by a lorry, Merckx because he was pulling the lorry!'

17

The stage win that was a death sentence

A helping hand: A seemingly absent minded Joaquim Agostinho takes a firm grip on Mogens Frey's handlebars in 1959.

The stage win that was a death sentence

'Turn it up! Turn up the volume, for heaven's sake. Can you hear what he's saying? Is Frey still leading?'

The commentator was speaking the French he had grown up with as fast as he could. He pronounced the name Mogens Frey in a way that no Dane would recognise but still there was no doubt. Mogens Frey had gone off alone and taken a four-minute lead over the Ballon d'Alsace, the giant of the Vosges that had been the Tour's first mountain right back in 1905.

'*Parlez moins vite!*' I hissed at the loudspeaker. Speak a little less quickly. French at that speed is far too fast. What right did the commentator have to overlook the possibility of Danes on a camping holiday?

Many Frenchmen had stopped to follow the race. One asked in Franglais if we were Danish. Damned right we were! So he offered to translate. This was 1970 and so far only one Dane had officially finished the Tour. The other, you'll remember, seems to have got as far as Paris but not into the paperwork. Now there was another in the race for the first time in ten years, in the little Frimatic team, and he'd taken this lead on the ninth stage in an attempt to climb all the mountains to Mulhouse.

The commentator recognised the paradox – a man from sea-level Denmark starring on a mountain. Researchers had brought him the little news of what Denmark had done before. He knew about Hans E Andresen's lonely way to the finish in 1958, and also about Arne Jonsson, who didn't even make the start because he'd lost his cycling shoes. He made us Danes feel important.

And then our Frenchman translated the awful news.

'I don't believe it,' our friend was gasping. 'They're saying that Joaquim Agostinho has gone after Frey – but it's his own team captain. It sounds totally mad.'

We Danes jumped as one. Who did this Portuguese think he was? These Mediterranean professionals, we sneered, they always did disapprove of our Nordic 'amateurs'. And yet they were the pure soul of cycling, the true cyclists. Why couldn't he leave Frey alone, let him win his stage?

We sipped nervously from our *café express*, we ordered more red wine, we nervously broke off bits of the *flûte* of bread and rolled dough balls. Frey and Agostinho. Agostinho and Frey. The two names, and a million French words, rattled from the radio.

'The Portuguese catches him. Frey is tired. He's sitting on his wheel and there are only a few kilometres to go. Is the Dane good enough in a sprint?'

'Oh yes,' we said, 'good enough to teach Agostinho a lesson, that's for sure. Oh yes!' But would he be allowed to? You're not supposed to sit on a wheel for a long time and then come sprinting past. And maybe there'd be trouble if you got to the finish with *monsieur le capitaine* and didn't let him win. Frey was professional enough to know he was in a double-sprung trap.

Except that with Frey you could never be sure. He was an unpredictable loner, the sort of man that a professional pecking order wouldn't tame. He had the form: silver at the Olympics, gold at the world championship. Why not the first Danish stage win in the Tour de France?

They passed under the kilometre-to-go triangle. Frey was still on Agostinho's wheel. The commentator returned to a speed we could follow. Frey took a short lead, then allowed himself to be caught. Now, said the commentator, he'd do the right thing and let his leader win. We shrugged.

Then the voice went into double-speed falsetto and we were lost.

'Frey is going. Frey is attacking. Agostinho is standing still. The Portuguese... Frey... *démarrage... et puis... alors... et maintenant... la ligne... il gagne... quoi?... de Gribaldy... le Danois...*'

What on earth was going on? Who'd won? Frey? The Portuguese out to ruin him?

Our French friend turned to us balefully: 'He was number two, *vôtre coureur*, but it was *drôle*, very strange. Your man, he attacked, but Agostinho took his *guidon*, his handlebars, and he pulled him back so that he was only second.'

'*WHAT???*'

He did what? What a...'

'*Salaud?*' our Frenchman suggested.

'What does he think this is, a kindergarten?'

The Frenchman continued to listen.

'Your man, he has gone to the commissaires and he is protesting with the arms and the legs. But his manager, he is trying to pull him away. Perhaps it is not yet decided. It is not permitted to pull at the bicycle of your *concurrent*.'

You bet it's not! Maybe in Portugal it was. But we want this decided by Danish rules.

And then: '*Eh bien! Il est déclassé...* Your man, he wins.'

We were on the Tour map. Denmark had won a mountain stage. We hugged our Frenchman. We drank a toast to the eccentric businessman Jean De Gribaldy, for his vision in signing Frey. The little grey-haired manager had a curious history in cycling. He called himself a nobleman, a count. But he knew a good Dane when he saw one, De Gribaldy. And it had been a double victory for Frimatic as well, despite the controversy.

We sent to the supermarket for wine and then we had an open house. The world was welcome to come and celebrate our Danish triumph. And maybe we'd even do it again; after all, there were still a couple of time-trials left in which Mogens would surely hold his own.

There was wine, cycling and bonding until the small hours. We napped then went blearily to buy *L'Equipe*. The scandal was everywhere. The French didn't see it quite the way we did, of course. Their interpretation was that Frey was weakening when Agostinho caught him. He'd paced the Dane to the finish and he should have been allowed to win. A cartoon showed them back to back with wiggly lines of coldness around them. The caption said '*Il fait Frey chez Frimatic.*' It was a play on the French for chilly weather – *il fait froid* – and a half-rhyme of the French pronunciation of Frey and the name of the team itself.

Relationships between Agostinho and the Danish hothead were chilled, the paper said. Frey had broken the rules. A *domestique* does not do things like that. By attacking his team leader, by protesting and getting the victory, by not knowing his place as a mere team rider, Mogens Frey had broken the unwritten laws of his profession. And he had signed his death warrant as a professional.

Il fait Frey chez Frimatic

Well, Frey finished just 59th in Paris but he had made Tour history. We Danes had a hard time forgiving Agostinho, whatever the professional justice on his side.

Eventually the Portuguese died as he lived, racing on his bike. He crashed when a dog ran in front of him. The story of his fracas with Mogens Frey tells us something important about the hierarchy of professional cycling and the danger of stepping out of line. I remember how proud we were at the time that a Dane had finally won a stage.

Only many years later did Danes reluctantly realise that maybe Agostinho was just a little within his rights to do what he did.

A moustache, poison and blue glasses

18

Sideman to an egotist

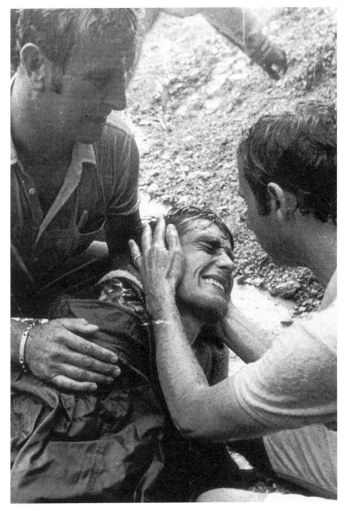

Battle scars: The Spanish star Luis Ocana suffers, after a fall, during his great duel in the Alps with Eddy Merckx in 1971. A winner of the Tour of Spain in 1970, Ocana went on to win the Tour in 1973.

Sideman to an egotist

I'll tell you another story about the hierarchy of professional cycling. Leif Mortensen was a superb rider, but he was probably too nice and too willing to help others to win the Tour himself. It's thrilling to see the dramatic happenings between Merckx and Ocana in 1971 through his eyes.

You'll remember that Merckx was the Cannibal, the man who won everything and devoured his rivals and their hopes. Well, nothing had changed. Merckx had already won Paris-Nice, Milan-San Remo, Liège-Bastogne-Liège and the Midi Libre and Dauphiné Libéré stage races.

He was coming to the 1971 Tour as the man who won emphatically the previous year. But there'd been interesting signs that he was human after all. He'd broken away and won on Mont Ventoux, but he'd been close to collapse. And emerging from the shadows was a Spanish novice with very obvious promise: Luis Ocana.

Bic's Maurice de Muer had built a strong team around Ocana with Mortensen as his right-hand man. Mortensen had been second in the Olympic road race in Mexico in 1968, won the world amateur championship the next year and had finished second in the professional championship in 1970. He was a fluent rider and just the mountain climber that a team leader needs.

Ocana had no respect for Merckx, a rivalry encouraged by Jacques Anquetil on French radio and by Raphaël Géminiani, whom De Muer had succeeded as team manager in 1970. Ocana's view was that any enemy of Merckx was a friend of his and he'd ride for anyone if there was a chance of harming the Belgian. Ocana had already shown in the Dauphiné Libéré that he had the talent to harass Merckx and he got to the Tour with a motivated team eager to inflict further damage.

Things started with promise. Ocana and Mortensen were involved when the field split and most of the favourites got 18 minutes on the second stage. After that Ocana followed Anquetil's radio advice and lay low through the lowlands.

Mortensen told me: 'We had an idea that Merckx's team wouldn't be so strong in the mountains. So the race started to get really interesting when we got to the Puy-de-Dôme. We attacked in shifts and Ocana finally went off alone. It got to be an incredible pursuit. At one point I felt I could get up to the group where Merckx was fighting to keep up, but Herman van Springel from his team was with me, so that idea was washed out.'

Ocana picked up 15 seconds on the Puy-de-Dôme but he must have felt they were 15 minutes. He interpreted them that way, anyway, and at the team's tactics meetings he started screaming that 'Merckx is soft! Attack, attack, attack!

He did just that. Two days later Merckx punctured on the stage to Grenoble and he took off. Merckx worked his way back through the team cars but the col de Porte was too hard and he got no nearer than 80 metres. The crowd, once so impressed, began to jeer.

'What on earth have I done to these people?' he wrote in his autobiography.

He lost a minute and 38 seconds on that stage and he was in danger. Géminiani told the press pointedly that 'Merckx must have very stiff legs after that pursuit' and De Muer needed no more encouragement. He laid battle plans. Battle plans that would operate from the first kilometres.

Bic's orange and white jerseys queued to attack. First was Charly Grosskost, a Frenchman who'd had huge promise as an amateur but never made the grade as a pro. It was an inexpensive move with great profit. Merckx panicked and used more of his team's energy than he needed on such a shrimp. One after the other, Bic wore Merckx down. Last but one was Mortensen and finally came Ocana.

The little Spaniard went from the bunch to the break and straight past without a glance. Merckx dropped behind his team and Mortensen right behind Merckx. Next day the papers reported that Mortensen had seen the hate in Merckx's eyes. It was a nice tale, but an exaggeration.

'He could very well have been extremely irritated at me, because I was the first person he saw every time he turned round', Mortensen recalled. 'But he also knew that I wasn't allowed to help. In fact just before the last climb most of us had no water left. When Merckx saw that, he passed his own bottle round his team-mates, then looked at me for a second and gave me the rest.

'That night Ocana came round to thank us all, but otherwise his only interest in his team-mates was professional. He was himself, he rode for himself, and he didn't worry about us if he could avoid it. On the other hand, you do have to admit that he had the ability to win!'

Ocana was beyond taming that day. He left Merckx for nine minutes to Orcières-Merlette. The Spaniard was on a high, his sparkling black hair parted neatly and his cap turned backwards as a greeting to anyone who dared follow him.

Merckx had called for a chase but the Tour ignored him. No one was going to help the Cannibal. He'd won so often by himself, now let him defend by himself. And without expression he did, he and his exhausted team tugging along the field far behind the Spaniard.

Real champions are great not just in their victories but in their defeats. And Merckx, now human, was as dignified in defeat as triumph. Géminiani, recalling the Judas Tour, said: 'There have been few efforts in history such as Ocana's, but I ask myself if Merckx isn't the more impressive, riding behind him with the whole field on his heels.'

That night, just as Merckx was being written off, rumours spread that he was down in the hotel garage, giving orders to the mechanics looking after his bikes. Something was up.

It was indeed. It began next morning when Bic riders were honoured on the podium at the start and therefore last to join the peloton. If Ocana could profit from Merckx's puncture then Merckx would punish that little conceit.

He went from the gun. The Bic team had to fight its way through the huge Tour peloton and get to the head of the race in pursuit of Merckx on the road to Marseille. How fortunes were reversed. Merckx regained two minutes in a fluent, inspired ride at 45kmh, won again next day in the mediaeval town of Albi, and he could then gaze south through the Midi haze at the distant smudge of the Pyrénées.

Merckx attacks furiously on the col de Mente, zigzagging from edge to edge to lose Ocana. Nothing helps. For the moment the sun is shining, the crickets are singing and all is as it should be on the mountains. But then they clear the peak and start the drop.

The other side is very different. It becomes hell's ride in the devil's weather. Filthy clouds fall and they can see no more than metres. A wave of rain and hail rakes across them. Wind buffets them and numbs their thighs. The narrow and dizzyingly steep road becomes a slippery mess.

Merckx leads, Ocana following. He sets a mad tempo through the hairpins and he loses control, crashing, falling into a low wall. Two spectators run to help as he picks up his bike and Ocana doesn't stand a chance. He rides straight into them.

A few riders pass and then, just as Ocana struggles to his feet, the Dutchman Joop Zoetemelk cannons straight into him, blinded by the rain. Then Agostinho and then Vicente Lopez-Carril. The others get up and continue but a helicopter takes Ocana to hospital with kidney pains. He's lost the Tour.

Merckx regained the lead again that evening but declined to wear the yellow jersey. He'd won it through misfortune, not talent. It was a matter of honour, another example of the Tour's private standards. A rider refused to wear the mountains jersey on the podium in 1998 when the previous holder lost it in a doping scandal. And in 1980 Zoetemelk rode without the yellow jersey for a day when tendinitis crippled Bernard Hinault.

The Tour passed through Ocana's home in Brittany some days later and Merckx visited Ocana on his sickbed. Ocana poured champagne and Merckx wished him victory in 1972. After that King Eddy was untouchable and he won his third Tour.

The col de Mente had been a nightmare for Leif Mortensen as well. Panic broke out after Ocana's crash. Maurice de Muer had seen how bad it was. He shouted at Mortensen to continue. If Ocana got up, against expectations, Mortensen could drop back to help. But for the moment Mortensen was team leader and de Muer needed him up the road.

The atmosphere in the Bic hotel was subdued that evening as the team waited for de Muer to return from hospital. He told them that Ocana lived but was badly hurt. He would give them the bonus they'd have received if Ocana had won in Paris. For the moment, though, Mortensen was fifth overall, he was to be given the help he needed, but more important was that Bic should keep its place as leading the team's competition. That was where publicity would come and therefore de Muer was looking for two or three riders at the front on every stage.

In Denmark, of course, they didn't know that. Nor would they have cared if they did. They saw Mortensen in fifth place and now the leader of his team. Why didn't he attack to get further ahead?

Mortensen says now: 'Of course, I always rode with that idea in my mind. It could have been good for me. But I always had to ride for the team's tactics.' And those tactics worked. Bic won the competition. Mortensen even won a prize as the most elegant rider. There was disappointment that he slipped a place on the last day. He punctured in the time-trial and Agostinho beat him by a couple of seconds.

Now let's jump 22 years to 1993 and put this all in perspective. Bjarne Riis was fifth and the Danish newspapers complained that he was getting too little support to keep or improve his position. Then Claudio Chiapucci attacked on the stage to Pau and suddenly all the Ariostea jerseys went to the front to work for Riis.

Positions changed and Riis finished alone by seven seconds. He kept his fifth place and Denmark could see that his team finally understood what it was worth. But there are other ways to see it.

Bernard Hinault answers questions every day in *L'Equipe*. One was: 'Didn't you feel sick, seeing the Ariosteas doing the yellow jersey's work just to save a place in the top ten?'

Hinault replied: 'It is incredible. Nothing can surprise me any longer on the Tour. But to ride like madmen just to save a fifth place seems a lightweight argument. Yesterday the team's energy should have been saved to fight for a better cause in the remaining days.'

Fifth place doesn't get you on the podium and it pays less than a stage win, less even than moving up in the team competition. But we Danes never considered that. All that mattered for us was

that another Dane was finishing the Tour and we wanted him one place better than Leif Mortensen in 1971.

Danish newspapers saw huge money in Mortensen's sixth place. Now he smiles wryly at headlines like 'MILLIONS FOR TOUR HERO.' He made money, yes, but hardly millions. Not even enough to put his feet up once he'd retired. And that despite Bic being a successful team. It won ten stage races in 1971 and Mortensen won the Trofeo Barracchi time trial with Ocana.

Bic wasn't as strong by 1973, although Mortensen did win the Tour of Belgium. The team abandoned him when he punctured on one stage and he had to get back alone. A few days later he got away with van Springel and won, which gave him the overall race.

Captain and his lieutenant: Luis Ocana (right) and Leif Mortensen.

The next weekend Mortensen had good legs in Paris-Roubaix. He was well placed but he crashed after a puncture. He fought back up to his 20-man group but by then it had broken up in the hell of cobblestones and punctures and shaken kidneys. He crashed again, got up, passed several others and glimpsed Walter Godefroot's group a hundred metres ahead.

The Bic team car was behind that group, not behind Mortensen. So he was defenceless when he punctured again. This time he pushed on with a flat tyre, even fighting off a challenge from Planckaert. It was one of the best rides of his life and he felt good despite the accidents.

A while afterwards he asked where Planckaert had finished.

'Sixth', said his mechanic. And then Mortensen realised he'd come fifth in Paris-Roubaix despite punctures, crashes and a flat, shredding tyre. And the three riders he'd been close to reaching were the three closest to Merckx, the winner.

If only... He took off his cap and hurled it into the mud in frustration. And then he looked at what he'd done.

'A souvenir! That's what I need, a souvenir.' So he picked up the cap, took it home and never washed it. It hangs now in the Hall of Fame in Copenhagen.

Merckx didn't ride the Tour in 1973 and Maurice de Muer showed no mercy. The Tour had to be won, preferably by Ocana but Mortensen would have the freedom to ride his own race. He had the strength to win if things fell right. He started well and he was third overall when it became clear just how strong Ocana was. Now Mortensen got fresh orders. Everybody was to ride for the Spaniard.

'It was irritating but de Muer was right,' Mortensen says now. 'Ocana did win. But de Muer was hopeless if ever there was even the slightest attack. He would order us to attack at the food stops. We were given extra food and then we took off when the others stopped for refreshments. It made us very unpopular.'

Then de Muer also fell out with the management.

'It was forbidden in the Tour to carry advertising on our jerseys. You could have the name of the team but nothing else. We had a logo that said 'Briquet Bic', Bic lighters, and that cost him 1,000 francs a man in fines each day.'

Ocana controlled the Tour as Merckx and Anquetil had in their own best years. He had the yellow jersey after the seventh stage and it was never in danger. Bic also won the team competition emphatically. Lieutenant Mortensen played a great part in the triumph but he never had the chance to improve on his sixth place in 1971.

19

An American in Paris

One for the boys back home: Greg LeMond and wife toast victory resting under the stars and stripes. LeMond's place in Tour history is special as he was the first non-European to win the Tour.

An American in Paris

An American? On the rostrum in Paris? Absurd! That was how the French saw it. They had no cycling culture 'over there'. Money was all that mattered to Americans. They took it where it was easy and they didn't want to suffer. No, the Americans would never win the Tour de France.

But then came Greg LeMond, so American with a name so French yet nobody knew how to say it. Was it *le monde?* Or 'lemon' as in English, or *limon* in French, maybe? And what about that 'd' at the end, and the capital M in the middle?

He won the world junior championship in 1979, turned professional in 1981, won the Tour de l'Avenir in 1982 and then became world champion in 1983, the year he also won the Super Prestige Pernod as the season's most consistent performer. He hadn't even ridden the Tour de France and yet he was the strongest American ever.

LeMond was to ride the Tour in 1984. America got behind him. Columbia took up its option to make a film with the Tour as background and Dustin Hoffman planned to train every day and follow the Tour in preparation.

The debut was impressive. A third place and white jersey as the best with less than three years as a professional. That was fine by the French. They liked a little novelty. The kid showed promise but he didn't interfere with the French view of their race, which was that it was disputed by Laurent Fignon and Bernard Hinault.

Hinault rode for the new La Vie Claire team, set up by the colourful French businessman Bernard Tapie. He wanted to win five times like Anquetil and Merckx but he'd been halted by Fignon, the winner in 1983. Fignon, a Parisian called 'the teacher' for his scholarly and lofty manner, rode with long blond hair tamed by a headband. He won three time-trials, left Hinault on the climb to Guzet Neige in the Pyrénées and then held him off through the Alps to make the road to Paris a triumphal procession.

LeMond, riding for Renault, had followed the best in the Alps and even outdistanced Hinault. Tapie was impressed and took him on for 1985. He needed LeMond for fear that he would become a danger in another team and in the meantime he could help Hinault. Meanwhile the Tour was over for Hoffman. He lost interest in the race and the project. Rumour insisted Sylvester Stallone would ride instead, even as Rambo. We should be grateful he didn't.

La Vie Claire dominated the Tour in 1985. Hinault and LeMond agreed to support whichever had the higher placing. Hinault won the prologue and a few days later the first time-trial and LeMond was locked, just as Tapie had planned. The businessman had political ambitions and being part of a national triumph would suit him fine. Fignon was no threat, affected by a crash, so the Tour became an internal dispute between two riders in the pay of a chain of health-food shops.

Hinault was no longer young, but he was clever. The Colombians in the race as part of its globalisation never put him in danger. Herrera won the mountain competition and two stages and Parra won the young riders' jersey, but that was the limit. Hinault did more damage to himself – he crashed a couple of days before the Pyrénées and broke his nose.

The crack made breathing difficult on his way to the Tourmalet. Stephen Roche, La Vie Claire's biggest threat, attacked. LeMond stuck on his wheel as the agreement and they disappeared into the clouds with Eduardo Chozas of Spain as company. Hinault was more than a minute behind when LeMond realised he was strongest of the three. He could win the Tour and Hinault could still be number two.

Up went his arm to call for Paul Koechli in the team car.

'I'm the strongest. I want to go.'

'No!' The answer was emphatic. LeMond knew why he'd been employed and what the agreement had been. Now he was being asked to stick to it and stay on Roche's wheel. He did it but he wasn't happy. He got off his bike in Luz Ardiden with a face as dark as his mood.

There was a heated discussion that night and Tapie soothed him.

'Bernard must defend his yellow jersey. A fifth victory would give him a place in history. You will win next year, I promise you that,' he said. And so it came to be. The year of Hinault and Tapie, everything in place and order. Except that LeMond later said he'd been lied to, that he'd been told he had 45 seconds instead of three to four minutes.

The USA was still not on the gold list but LeMond had finished third and second and he'd been promised the race in 1986. Back in the States, the film was resuscitated, this time with Ryan O'Neal. He'd be as handsome as Hugo Koblet, Raymond Poulidor or a young Hinault, but he need never be in France. Helicopters, motorbikes and cars carried cameras to record the Tour and Ryan would act his part in Hollywood. The footage was shot by Jorgen Leth, who made *Sunday in Hell*, the film of Paris-Roubaix, and *Stars and Water-carriers*. They are incredible pictures but they've never been shown. Will we have to wait for ever?

Hollywood is a commercial operation. Perhaps now after Armstrong's win in 1999? The Tour and team sponsorship are also commercial operations. They don't always attract the sweetest characters. Bernard Tapie didn't become a hero through Hinault but he did as chairman of the French soccer team Olympique Marseille. And then it turned to ashes. Evidence was found of bribery in the European Cup final, he was convicted and went to prison. A populist with no respect for the traditions of sport or its sportsmen, he supported cycling simply to elevate himself.

Many suspected he would have preferred Hinault to win in 1986. Had he discussed that with Hinault? Is that what Hinault meant when he said: 'I will help Greg but only so long as he shows himself worthy of the yellow jersey'?

Hinault saw to it that LeMond was seen to be worthy. He won less time than expected from the young American in the prologue and the time-trials but he continued to behave as team captain, directing the action. An evil mind could interpret that as a war against LeMond.

Hinault attacked on the first day in the Pyrénées with such intensity that he split the field. Only the Spaniard Pedro Delgado could follow him, going on to win the stage. LeMond lost four minutes and Fignon the whole race. He finished the day with a fever, 11 minutes down, and quit.

Hinault was on the warpath again on the day the race went over the Tourmalet and the col d'Aspin to Superbagnères. But this time he broke himself. And LeMond broke everybody else to take the yellow jersey.

Five days later came the stage over the Galibier and the Croix-de-Fer to Alpe d'Huez. It would be LeMond's test of worthiness. Hinault led throughout. He pedalled like a maniac. But LeMond wouldn't be drawn. At the front, the kaleidoscope jersey of La Vie Claire, behind it, the yellow of the leader. A train with one engine and a carriage, but with the driver trying to unhook his train.

Tapie couldn't have asked for better advertising for his company or himself. A double triumph in the greatest event in cycling. A sixth victory for Hinault would ice the cake. The two stayed together until the finish. Thousands on the mountain and millions before their television screens saw LeMond push up alongside Hinault just before the line and put his arm around his shoulders for a moment as if to say 'I could win this now – but I won't.' Then he let Hinault cross the line first.

It could bring tears to your eyes. It was beautiful, just beautiful. Hinault explained that he had passed on the sceptre and given his young replacement the Tour de France. LeMond stayed passive and gave nothing away. But finally he explained: 'On the climb, Hinault had asked for one last victory. He said 'You are the strongest but can I please lead to the top just one more time?''

He was hurt when he heard the way the Frenchman put it, that it was a gift almost from father to son. So hurt that he opened up further.

'I should just have gone myself. I could easily have taken five minutes. I have since learned to see through Hinault and his type.'

Years later he added: 'It almost burned me out of cycling, that little episode. I didn't even feel like racing the following year. It was like being burned by your brother. The thing is that Hinault wasn't your typical team-mate. He was a guy I idolised.' Relations between the two have since been neutral at best.

No one could deny the American victory in Paris. And how did he celebrate? By being photographed in his hotel room, lying in bed in his La Vie Claire jersey and a black bow tie. An American flag covered the bed with its stars and stripes and his wife poured him champagne. The French shook their heads. Anquetil and Merckx would never have done that. They were crazy, those Americans.

And the film? Well, they gave up again. Kilometres of thrilling celluloid gather dust on American shelves somewhere. Jorgen Leth's efforts to have them released have failed.

LeMond, too, nearly became history. His brother-in-law shot him accidentally on a hunting trip near Sacramento the following April. LeMond lay in a coma for two weeks with serious internal and external injuries, in grave danger. Nobody expected him on a bike again, but you don't win the Tour if you can't suffer. He began training again in September, which he now concedes was too soon.

'Nearly 60 per cent of my blood volume was gone and that takes months to get back,' he said. 'I remember going back to Europe at the end of August and only being able to make it one mile into a race. I was doing it because under my contract with PDM it was contingent that I would start racing again in '88. Plus my contract with La Vie Claire required that I race x number of days in '87. If I hadn't raced again that year, they would have been able to cancel my contract. So I was forced to go back.'

It was painful but to everyone's amazement he turned up in the Giro d'Italia in 1989. Most felt sorry for him. Imagine having been the world's best and then to be humiliated. There were still lead pellets in his body. He had no appendix; his liver and kidneys were permanently damaged. It was an impossible task. The Giro was not a success yet he came through it.

Later he said that only then did he realise what real suffering was – a pain that, once surmounted, led not to the podium but to a victory over one's self.

The year 1989 was to prove a good vintage, with bouquet and substance. The drama began even before the race started. Pedro

Delgado was so happy signing autographs that he 'forgot' to go to the prologue and lost 2:54 before turning a pedal. In Rennes, LeMond shocked by winning the first big time-trial in front of Delgado and Fignon, and then again by speaking a drawling American French that nobody had heard before. He'd used his two wasted years to learn it and the last sceptical Frenchmen gave in. This was a good man, they said, almost French even, and many hoped that he and not Fignon would win. And what a duel was in store before that was settled.

Delgado tried desperately to become involved, but he failed when Fignon pulled himself from a crisis on the Tourmalet, attacked up to Superbagnères and turned what could have been defeat into the yellow jersey.

Five days later LeMond claimed the jersey by winning the team time-trial in Orcières-Merlette. Then, Delgado attacked on the Alpe d'Huez but cracked five kilometres from the top to Fignon. The Frenchman rode by without looking back, his ponytail flapping, and became leader again. He attacked again next day so illogically that the bunch was stunned and he won the stage. His lead now seemed decisive but there was still the time-trial on the last day. LeMond was not yet beaten, as he showed when he won the last mountain stage.

The difference at the start of the time-trial into Paris was 50 seconds. The race was only 24.5km. You remember the great battle between Poulidor and Merckx? Now it was Fignon and LeMond and a similarly spellbound audience. The difference this time was that the stronger man was coming from behind.

LeMond averaged 54.545kmh, the fastest ever for a Tour time-trial longer than 20km. For Fignon the race was 500m too far. He lost the Tour by an agonising eight seconds. He'd ridden 3,285km to be beaten by eight measly seconds!

LeMond let out a whoop when the clock passed his time. He hugged everyone around him and even officials from the American embassy opposite the finishing line forgot their diplomatic dignity and yelled with him.

Later that year, he won the world championship for the second time. What a resurrection for a man so close to death. His health still stopped his participating in the full season and so he concentrated on just the Tour and the world championship. It brought him much criticism from people, Eddy Merckx among them, who felt a star showed disrespect by not giving himself to all the great classics.

In reality, LeMond was ahead of his time. Now everybody realises it's impossible to be in peak condition all year. The only exception, perhaps being Laurent Jalabert, who advanced from sprinter to complete rider in the Tour de France of 1995 and later won almost everything. He's a second cannibal of a sort, going for wins the whole season.

LeMond won the Tour a third time in 1990 after a hectic chase when four strong riders were allowed ten minutes on the first stage. The hardest to catch was Chiapucci, dethroned only on the last but one day in the time-trial at Lac de Vassivières. LeMond took the yellow jersey again in 1991, but he was no longer king. The crown had passed to Miguel Indurain, Delgado's lieutenant of the previous two years, and he'd reign for a further five years before cracking in the mountains and leaving the sport.

Another era had passed.

20

When Riis got
the measles

A pair of 'Great' Danes:
A great favourite with the fans, Jesper Skibby (left) with the 1996 Tour winner Bjarne Riis.

When Riis got the measles

Get rid of that umbrella and come in here. It's a good thing we've got the Tour to watch now that July's about to set records for rainfall. Come on... it's starting in a moment.

Right, sink into a chair by the table. Everything's ready – coffee, Coke, cans of beer, family-size packets of sweets, crisps and dips. The house shrine is tuned to the cycling channel. It's 1.54pm on July 10, 1993.

The stage is just right for Jesper Skibby to win, just like the day before yesterday. Or what about Rolf Sørensen? He's desperately hungry to win.

It's starting. These have to be the best graphics ever. A line worms its way to music over a map of France and marks the day's route from Péronne to Châlons-sur-Marne. A picture of the race leaders follows: Cipollini in yellow, Nelissen in green, and Bjarne Riis's team-mate Cassani in the polkadot mountain jersey. At last: the first pictures from the helicopter. Seven men in a break through the rolling French countryside. The camera zooms in.

It's Riis. That forehead is difficult to miss. The faster he got as a cyclist, the more the wind took his hair. But it could be Leanizbarrutia. His hair's just the same. But then he rides for ONCE and this is an Ariostea jersey, so it must be Riis. Let's try to hear who's there with him.

The commentators on TV2 in Denmark are the poetical film man Jorgen Leth and the journalist Jørn Mader. They're explaining that Riis has won the last three mountain sprints and is close to the polkadot jersey. What? If Riis has won those three sprints then he is already the mountain leader, surely? Haven't they seen that two of the climbs are higher category and therefore give more points? He and Cassani may be even if Cassani won the first sprint, but that would mean Riis needed just one more point in the final sprint and there you have it.

A Dane in polkadots! How about that?

Maybe we should hold off trying to be smarter than Leth and Mader. I'm sure they can add a couple of mountain points together. And now let's see who's with Riis.

Well, it's a good break, but Johan Museeuw's in it. He and not Riis will take the yellow jersey if the break stays together. And he'll probably also win the sprint. But there are 78km to the finish and anything can happen.

Oh no! Now I see there are three from Motorola. Let's look. One is Mejia and he's more of a mountain rider, so he doesn't count. And Riis has Cenghialta from Ariostea with him. I can recognise Sierre from his dark hair and his headband, but he's a climber too. Phil Anderson, though, he could be dangerous if he's allowed to get away.

And Anderson looks strong. He's got a grin that could make a racoon tumble from a tree. Just like Davy Crockett. Give the man a gum shield!

Max Sciandri is also dangerous, and he looks good, too. Look at that lovely wavy hair, not the slightest ruffled after all those kilometres.

'I wonder what he's doing tonight?', says one of the girls.

'Sleeping,' comes the answer from along the room. 'What else do you think cyclists do at night? You probably also think it's vanity that stops his wearing a helmet. Well, neither does Riis or Cenghialta, and nor does Mejia. That's 4-3 to the helmet-less.'

We munch through the sweets, dip crisps, drink the beer, Coke and coffee. Who cares if it's raining out there so long as Riis can do what Skibby did and cheat them all?

The weather's better in France, I see. Solid cumulous stands like pillars and makes the sky half-overcast. It's slightly windy but it's dry enough for dust clouds between the expansive vineyards that sit among the woods and the fields of corn and hay. From time to time the riders pass through typical French towns of grey houses built from blocks of stone. Tens of thousands of Frenchmen line the route. We can hear their applause.

The field is calm. It fills the width of the road, keeping the speed down. Indurain and Roche are cosy, and I get a glimpse of Cipollini in yellow.

Whoops! Riis has a problem. We quiver with worry as he changes his front wheel. He's back in the saddle in an instant. The service car is just ahead and he can use it to pace him back. Leth and Mader commiserate. Riis is riding so well that the others will wait for him. Yes, but will he make it before the mountain sprint or use so much energy that he'll lose if he does get back?

We stop biting our nails. Riis reaches them. He takes it easy at the back and then takes the lead on the climb. He accelerates hard a few hundred metres before the finish. Museeuw doesn't react. His interest lies in the two later sprints where he can pick up more seconds towards the yellow jersey. That's his goal for the day.

From the helicopter we see Riis win the mountain sprint. It's in the bag. The first Dane in the spotted jersey. Unbelievable. That Riis is turning into something special. It's what Fignon has been saying all along: Riis is stronger than he realises. Slowly Riis finds this out for himself. He gives his all in the break. Ariostea's car is there with drinks. Museeuw is also giving it everything. His car is also alongside, his manager more than half out the window as he gesticulates instructions.

The three Motorola riders, with an M on their backs, start to pull away. There are enough of them for a good chance of winning. Sierra hangs with them a little, but not too much. It's the perfect break. More than three minutes' advantage.

A new town. The name appears on the screen: Fleury-la-Rivière. Wow! We'll remember this one. What decorations. Numerous and varied banners hang across the road, a meter-high cyclist covered in flowers stands by the road and a huge banner reads VIVE LE TOUR DE FRANCE 1993 just before the field leaves town. The next town. What's this one called? The caption appears. *Tête de la course* it says. Oh.

The course now follows the Marne. Long, grey stone walls enclose the wineries. Policemen wave yellow flags to show the right way round roundabouts. Sierra's not doing well now. It's getting hard and he's repeatedly pouring water over himself.

The ONCE team moves to the front of the chasers, starting to pull away. The break's lead is coming down. Museeuw accelerates and wins, picking up six seconds, and the group splits for a moment.

'They'd bloody well not let that sprint ruin their co-operation,' I mutter. Sciandri and Museeuw obviously hear me and, wisely, they agree. They shout and wave at the others, irritated. Harmony is re-established.

Conversation is still lively, but the excitement is increasing and we're careful not to drown out the television. Twenty kilometres to go and 2:50 to the break. And then some good news from Leth and Mader. It's an admission.

'We have now become wiser,' one of them says. 'Two third-category mountains had sneaked in, so Riis has more points. He's got 44, Cassani 39. So we have the first Dane in a mountain jersey.'

I chuckle.

'What did I tell you?' I shout at the television set. Unbelievable that they can't do their homework. 'Is it really that hard to see from the route map whether a mountain is a category three or four?' Then I calm down. Well, they do have other things to think about.

'Maybe you know as much about the castles along the route as Leth does?' someone says.

Ten kilometres to the finish. It's still 2:37. It must be enough. Mader says two Danish wins in the first seven stages would be almost too much. Why? If Riis wins, I guarantee you it won't be long before Sörensen takes another stage.

The Motorola guys ride like madmen. Riis is stuck at the back, as if he had a red light on the yellow and red diagonal stripes of his Ariostea jersey. Maybe he's having a hard time. More likely he's sitting there to see everything. He's ice-cool like that, Riis. He's also ridden hard earlier on. It's only reasonable to let Museeuw work a little harder for his yellow jersey.

Four kilometres to go. Riis is still at the back. He empties his pockets. Every gram counts in the final sprint. The camera moves on to Anderson's perfect teeth, bared and clenched like a horse. A million dentists all over Europe put up a cheer.

The rest of the sweets go down without tasting of anything. There's no more conversation, just exclamations.

'Did you see that?...'

'There goes Mejia!...'

'Only six for the sprint...'

Riis is still last.

'Maybe he's learned a little patience,' says Leth.

Well frankly he can't do anything else. He's dead-tired but his will is immovable. He's had the best legs of the day. Museeuw has slaved for the last 20km. Why shouldn't Riis win? Then he gets locked. His team-mate, Cenghialta, takes off with just about a kilometre to the finish.

'Oh no! Please don't let it last!'

And it doesn't. Cenghialta is caught, falls behind resignedly, clips a motorcycle and crashes. The front riders don't see it. Riis sits perfectly on Museeuw's wheel. Museeuw is pulled forward by Sciandri. Riis sees an opening to the right, takes advantage of being in the highest gear and shoots off along the finish straight and wins.

He won! Riis won!

We jump in excitement. Oh my God, this man is good! Anything can happen now. Just wait and see on Isola 2000. Watch out Indurain – Denmark is coming! The 56 bells in the churches of Châlons-sur-Marne ring out for Bjarne Riis.

Leth says: 'He has really developed as a rider.' That is very true. I wonder what the limit is. Maybe he will become as strong as Leif Mortensen. Admiration pours from the TV set. Denmark, little Denmark, has won two of the first seven stages. Leth and Mader tell us that these two victories make Denmark the dominant nation.

It is almost a dream. It may be raining outside but in that little box over there Riis is first on the podium and taking flowers as the winner of the stage. Then he has to come back for the polkadot jersey. And overall he is fourth.

This has to be celebrated, and it will be. Châlons-sur-Marne has made sure he won't forget where he won. It's in the Champagne district and it's set aside 200 bottles for the winner.

Riis is all but mown down by reporters on his way to the podium. Many are Danish and so Riis speaks only Danish. It angers one of the French journalists so much that he climbs the barriers and starts to climb to the podium with Riis. He gets into a fight with a couple of policemen before being dragged off.

And then there was Jesper Skibby's reaction to seeing his countrymen covered in red spots.

'Has Riis got the measles?' he said.

What happened next? Well, Riis lost the mountain jersey next day, but a couple of days later he rode his way over Isola 2000 and into the panoply of Tour favourites. Folk started to call him the Eagle of Herning, and as you probably know in 1996 Riis won the Tour.

Herning, by the way, is as flat as a pancake.

A moustache, poison and blue glasses

21

The Tour of death

The memorial to Fabio Casartelli: The descent of the Col de Portet d'Aspet in 1995 saw the tragic death of the 1992 Italian Olympic road-race champion. This climb of the Pyrénées was part of the first mountain stage of the Tour in 1910.

The Tour of death

'Crash! Crash! Motorola... Museeuw, Perini!' The news broke through Radio Tour on July 18, 1995. There are many crashes, but this was clearly different. The Italian, Fabio Casartelli, lay unconscious in the road. Blood streamed from his head. Others clutched lesser injuries but Casartelli wasn't moving.

Gérard Porte, the race doctor, shouted for a helicopter. Casartelli, the Olympic champion in Barcelona, was 24. He had a six-month-old son. And Porte gave him little chance as he looked down on him on the way to hospital. Casartelli's skull was broken and he was bleeding inside. His heart stopped three times. Hospital doctors tried for two hours to revive him. And then he died.

The announcement was made in the middle of a dramatic stage. The organisers let the race continue. Critics said it was because Richard Virenque, a Frenchman, was trying to repeat his triumph in the Pyrénées in 1994. The Tour denied it. Up front, the leaders heard nothing. They were fighting for seconds and minutes right to the final metre. But the bunch heard and it stopped racing and limped to the finish.

Jesper Skibby reached the finish half an hour after the leaders. The cameras watched as he asked his soigneur 'Was it his head?' The soigneur nodded and Skibby put his fingers to his eyes to stem the emotion. French television knew he must have seen the crash and that it would have brought back memories of his own accident in Tirreno-Adriatico in 1993. His fate could have been the same.

'The road is probably too dangerous,' he said. 'It's a right-angled bend and it's misleading. There was no fencing. Someone hit a concrete pillar and then the Motorola rider (Casartelli) crashed. Fifty kilometres from the finish we heard he was dead and we stopped racing. Suddenly you realise just how little it all matters. The stage should never have been finished. It hurts particularly because I've been through it myself.'

Casartelli was the third rider to die in the Tour's 92 years. Many, indeed, thought the race should have stopped. The organiser, Jean-Marie Leblanc, said everything that needed to be said: the Tour had sent its condolences to Casartelli's young widow, Marie. She would get all the help she needed, financial, psychological and practical. The Tour would pay for the funeral and Bernard Hinault would be there to mourn along with Jean-Claude Killy from the Tour's management.

Motorola decided to continue. There was a minute's silence before the next day's race.

But then it came: 'The race was magnificent today and deserves normal attention for Virenque's incredible performance and the efforts so many others made in the colossal confrontations. That should not be forgotten because of something that happens at the other end of the race. The show must go on.'

It cut to the heart. And worse, it was just the start of days of poor taste. It began with the announcement. Then viewers began ringing television stations to complain that they hadn't seen the actual crash. They demanded the pictures. Well, no cameras were there when Casartelli fell. So television compromised by lingering on the dead man for 20 seconds as he lay in a bag on the freezer shelf of his mortuary. It was macabre.

L'Equipe next day showed a cartoon cyclist riding a mountain to heaven as a spectator shouts: 'It's Fabio!'

The riders were horrified. Rumours spread of a go-slow in Casartelli's memory and as a protest.

It should have been the second hardest stage. Pau is only 30km from Tarbes but the Tour was going on a detour over some of the highest mountains in the Pyrénées, and that in scorching sun. The distance that way was 234km.

Motorola was first to be called to the start, then the three leaders in their jerseys, and finally the rest of the 119 who survived from 189 starters. They climbed the mountains like snails. Motorola riders won the first sprints. Nobody left the race through its pace. The only dropouts were from trouble with bikes or the heat.

The race was an hour and a half late at the finish. The Italian, Davide Cassani, had gone to Richard Virenque and suggested that Motorola should take every prize and the stage should be neutralised. Virenque agreed and everyone fell into step. Not that they all agreed. It suited Banesto (Miguel Indurain) and ONCE (Alex Zülle) that the year's last hard stage should be scrapped. It denied Riis his last chance to attack before the time-trials.

Riis himself saw it differently.

'We won't feel any better for riding eight hours thinking about our dead colleague,' he said. 'That kind of thing should be forgotten as quickly as possible, but of course I am united with the others. And maybe I am also bitter. The stage would have been incredibly hard and I was ready to attack Zülle again.'

The Motorola riders moved to the front as the rest dropped back in the streets of Pau. A moved audience clapped as the blue jerseys held each other's shoulders before the finish, then separated again so that Casartelli's friend, Andrea Peron, could cross the line first.

All the prize money went to Casartelli's widow. There was agreement that the Tour had demonstrated unity, solidarity and sensitivity. *L'Equipe* wrote: 'A beautiful gesture. Something that shows that we all belong to one big cycling family. A magnificent and almost spontaneous reaction from a united field.'

There was debate about whether a helmet could have saved Casartelli, but not even his fate makes riders use one. Cyrille Guimard, the great old rider and now manager of Castorama, said: 'If you crash at 65kmh, it doesn't matter whether you're wearing a helmet or not.'

Laurent Jalabert said: 'Most of us think about it the day after such an accident, but (wearing a helmet) is both impractical and uncomfortable.'

Jesper Skibby was quoted at the start of the next day's stage before he knew of the united action: 'I will not ride with a helmet from the start, but I will bring one with me – you can be sure of that'... and yet he was quick to give it up again with a typical reply (gently mocking a country infamous for it's restrictions on individualism) 'We don't live in Sweden!'...

22

Rockin' round the clock

At home on the podium: Miguel Indurain steps off the podium after his first Tour victory in 1993. He would be back on it again!

Rockin' round the clock

The sun is last to get up. A lot has happened on the Tour before it stretches and yawns its way above the horizon. Huge lorries are being emptied of the metal rods that will make the grandstands and the temporary offices at the finish. The police are fencing the finishing area and barriers are going up along the run-in. The press centre is beginning to fill with tables and chairs and rows of televisions.

Out on the road, dangerous sections are secured with barriers and markings. Junctions are closed for hours in advance. Cars stop at intervals to erect banners. There's advertising for the sponsors and for radio and television stations broadcasting the Tour. Signs show the bonus and mountain sprints and the distance to the finish. The great gate that holds the kilometre-to-go triangle is inflated over the road.

The start has been sectioned off since the middle of the night. Another area, *Le Village*, stands ready. It holds the same features every day but it's always different, according to local conditions. One morning it stands in beautiful countryside with lawns and small lakes. The next it could be in a dark and cavernous exhibition hall. *Le Village* is an exclusive place where the Tour's accredited followers can relax before the start. Riders slip by for a drink or some fruit after they've signed on. They read the papers or to talk to journalists. Reporters collect plastic bags of papers from the yellow stand of Crédit Lyonnais, each bag printed with the number of the journalist's badge.

The fair-haired girls in yellow solve all problems and speak all the languages. Among them are the kissing girls who'll pull the jerseys over the day's leaders. They're picked from many different nations from hundreds of applicants. It helps to be pretty – long blond hair is an advantage – clever and strong.

Breakfast is a buffet of bread, fruit, finger-food and the region's specialities. Breakfast is a gastronomic tour of the country, fish by the sea, spicy sausage in the mountains, sickeningly sweet but tempting cakes in many of the towns.

Registration for each stage takes place outside *Le Village*. It's usually in a square with a grandstand. Riders have an hour to prove by their signature that they're riding. Thousands know this is the place to cheer heroes and everyone is applauded.

The announcer, Daniel Mangeas, has done the job for 25 years here and at other classic races. He introduces each rider properly. No one is ever allowed to think that there may be *weak* riders in the Tour de France. Everyone is a hero to Mangeas.

Coca-Cola is one of the main sponsors, along with Crédit Lyonnais, Champion and Fiat. It arranges the American cheerleaders. They practise complicated routines and dances as though they were at the Super Bowl. They're chosen for their talent rather than their looks; several overflow their red outfits and prompt jokes about strengthening the stands. But can they dance! They swing pom-poms in perfect synchronisation.

The advertising caravan sets off an hour before the riders. There are fantastic figures everywhere. Companies promote themselves by throwing samples to the crowd.

The town is full of cars. Parking plans make sure everyone can set off at the right time. Journalists and officials who have to reach the finish before the riders queue up *en avant*, ahead of the field. They can then follow the Tour route to the finish, getting an impression of what's in store for the riders, or take shortcuts suggested in the race bible, an instruction manual with all sorts of practical information.

Morning meeting place:
Le Village is a colourful and interesting part of the Tour, where riders mingle with the sponsors, media and organisers over coffee before each stage start

157

Several hundred blue police motorcycles drive in front, among and behind the riders. They are an impressive sight lined up. They remind you that 13,000 officers and 3,500 security guards make the Tour run smoothly. It's impressive to see policemen guarding even the smallest tractor paths from 6am to allow the race free passage. They're dedicated to every detail, even when the sun bakes them in the hours before the riders pass.

Eventually the huge field gathers. The Tour caravan is a kilometre long and it starts to move off slowly. Cyclists, race officials, service cars, radio and television journalists, it's several minutes before everyone has left. And the moment they have, the loudspeakers at *Le Village* emit a loud noise followed by the announcement that 'We close in five minutes.'

Nobody can sit and contemplate the leftovers for the rest of the day. Exactly five minutes later, it's over. The village is broken down and carted to the next start.

There's traffic chaos around the Tour. The barriers create long queues up to 50km away. The Tour cars, the technicians and the accredited journalists must get through, and they do – usually with pedals hard to the floor. They slalom through lampposts, dodge on and off pavements, ride against oncoming traffic. Most countries' drivers would stand by their rights, but in France everyone gives way to the Tour. It's in their blood.

Motorists pull to the side as though fire engines were on the way. The police make it easier. There are no driving fines. Few of those whizzing along appreciate nature's glory around them, the estuaries on the west coast, the snow-topped mountains in the Alps, the burning gold of giant sunflowers towards Toulouse. But they remember when they get home and then they yearn to go back and look at them all in peace.

Each metre of the Tour is accounted for and described in detail, even before the route is confirmed a year in advance. Every rider gets a description of each stage so that he can plan his race. Names of regions and towns, times for passing landmarks at various speeds, dangerous sections and all the refreshment stops, they're all shown.

The rules for the riders' feeding zones are strict. They can get their food and drink only from the correct people in the correct areas, or from their team cars. It's in the riders' interests. Only zoo animals have food passed to them by spectators. And limits on food and drink lessen the chance of poisoning and unwanted substances appearing.

Thousands gather along the roads. There are battles for the best vantage points, like the steepest mountains. Touring cyclists and amateur racers try the climbs themselves in the days before the race. Many spectators set up camp the day before the race in tents or in vans covered with stickers. Cyclists from the same country form villages and write their heroes' names on the road and put up flags and banners before having a hefty breakfast to prepare for their wait.

French café life buzzes in towns large and small. The race is discussed eagerly over espresso and wine. One ear listens to the radio for news. There are even reports on the French Minitel system and on the internet.

The press centre comes to life at the finish. A thousand journalists sit at long tables as if they were eating school dinners. They watch French television. There are many advantages to speaking French in France. Most French people know nothing else or, if they do, refuse to speak it.

A rush breaks out when thousands of small cans of Fanta and Coca-Cola arrive at the huge freezers. It's important to get a good cache because they'll run out, however many were put there. The same applies to bottles of Vitel water. They always run out.

Stories are sent all over the world from a little neighbouring room that contains everything in communication. It's cheaper to use the buses of telephones and faxes outside the press centre but you need a phone card.

A huge number of media people arrive and leave during the Tour and each must pass through the permanence bus. The deadline for accreditation is early – February 1 – but it means everything is ready when the journalists arrive. Strict rules govern who can be accredited. There can be 3,500 people travelling with the Tour and to let the numbers get out of hand would be chaotic. Some already have to drive more than 100km to find their hotels.

Alongside the *permanence* bus is the Tour's post car. You can send your mail there all day, all specially postmarked. Letters arrive every morning and evening from all over the world, mostly to the riders. All you have to do is write, for instance, Chris Boardman, Tour de France, and it will reach him.

The best idea is to address your letter to a stage town four or five days ahead. It will get there by *dynaposte* and the four people in the *dynaposte* car will not only deliver the mail but keep a record of who gets most.

An obstacle course lies between the press centre and the finish line. Stalls sell souvenirs, buses arrive to take riders to their hotels, cars and vans stand about from the broadcasting stations, and the ground is a maze of cables. A single gap in the fence lets journalists out to the course.

The spectators fill one side of the road. The victory podium and the TV and radio cubicles are on the other, right before the line. The commentators are cramped, but they do have plenty of information, including descriptions of buildings the race will pass and their architects, references to museums and natural attractions. The book is wonderful if there are moments of inactivity to fill.

Further down the line is the doctor's cabin, where riders call for drug checks and anyone can visit for treatment.

Here are the VIP stands, where the main sponsors entertain business contacts, politicians and friends. Then the riders blast by. The journalists face a hard job getting the ones they want if they finish in a group. Deadlines are always too close.

There's a man in a Volkswagen van who runs his own Tour de Tricot. He gets busy as soon as the field passes. This is the man who looks after the jerseys that will be pulled over the heads of the competition winners. It's no coincidence they always have the right size and logos. He doesn't have a big supply of jerseys and team patches but he does have the heights and widths of the whole field. He checks the result against his list, takes the right jerseys, finds the right logos and makes up whatever's needed. In the old days climbers drowned in jerseys designed for sprinters and the brawny were squeezed into jerseys made for lightweights. Now it can happen only if the teams give the wrong information or Monsieur de Tricot misreads the numbers.

Back in the press centre, journalists drown in information, all in stacks of paper. The result of the stage, overall positions, results of sprints and mountain competitions, standings for the green jersey, the polkadot and the under-25s competition. There are medical reports: whom the doctor treated during the day and for what, right down to drops of iodine for scratches.

The barriers are already being dismantled and sent on. Riders are having their sore muscles treated on massage tables at their hotel before eating and planning the next day's tactics. Everybody else celebrates through the night, helping bars and restaurants to giant profits.

Paris celebrates the final stage on the Champs-Elysées. Every rider who finishes has achieved something special and he's cheered on a lap of the long and beautiful tree-lined boulevard. And then it's all over for a year.

It's three weeks' labour for the officials and journalists. For them it's over. But for the riders there's just a night of relaxation, perhaps a bottle of champagne, and then they're off to local races all over Europe where they'll be the stars of the day.

Next year is on the way. And in the Tour's offices in the Parisian suburb of Issy-les-Moulineaux, someone will already know how many barriers, how many jerseys, how many hotels, how many fax machines, how many...

A moustache, poison and blue glasses

23

Too good to be true

All smiles:
Director of the Tour,
Jean-Marie Leblanc
(left) and the new
'All American Hero'
Lance Armstrong
after his astounding
victory.

Too good to be true

The executive of the Hollywood film company leaned towards his enthusiastic young guest: "Young man, I know nothing of sports, and I never thought I would ever be thinking of making a movie about a sports star but you are talented and have surprised me before. I will listen to you. Go on!"

Thanks. I am sure that you will realise just how visual a sport cycling is, the drama, the tension that builds up and under which exceptional circumstances this man has achieved his results.

His name is Lance Armstrong. Born in Plano, a suburb of Dallas, Texas, 18 September 1971, he later moved to the capital, Austin, where he soon showed great talent for sports, becoming a promising triathlete. His particular talent however, was cycling and specialising in that, as a 19 year old he won the US Amateur Road Championship and was considered a gold medal candidate for the road race at the Barcelona Olympics 1992 not only by others but also very much by himself.

When he finished 14th he was bitterly disappointed and even thought of quitting but changed his mind and instead signed a professional contract with the American Motorola team. Shortly afterwards he made his debut in Clasica San Sebastian, one of the season's great World Cup events. A complete fiasco. He had sworn that he would complete the race no matter what happened, and he did... He finished last and learned immediately just how tough professional cycling is but promised himself he would be back.

Unperturbed by this career low, he fought his way upwards, with support not only from his team, but also from his mother Linda, who always believed in him. If others did not they were soon forced to change their minds. The career of the biggest cycling name in US-history, Greg LeMond, was over. Now everybody was looking for a new star. It might be Armstrong, who two weeks later finished 2nd to Viatscheslav Ekimov, the lone winner, in the Grand Prix of Zurich, another of the World Cup races, won a stage in Tour of Galicia and came first in the Grand Prix Sanson.

1993 was a first career high. A special bonus of one million dollars had been put up for a rider who won three events in the

Tour of America: the Pittsburgh Thrift Drug Classic, the K-Mart Classic stage race and the US Professional Championship. Armstrong dominated these events in style with great help from a devoted team which had their piece of the million dollar cake.

The opposition was stronger in Europe, though, and he was scheduled to start in the Tour de France but had to withdraw ahead of the mountains. This did not prevent him from being close to one stage win in a solo escape, after which he won stage 8, the stage to Verdun a few days later in a terrific sprint. By becoming the youngest ever rider at 21 to win a stage of the Tour de France, people naturally began to ask him if he considered himself to be "the second Greg LeMond" and they all got the same answer: No, I am the first Lance Armstrong!

Despite these successes nobody believed that he would be a medal candidate at the World Road Race Championship in Oslo, Norway. Featuring many riders who would later dominate the Tour de France – Jan Ullrich, a Tour-winner to be in 1997, won the amateur race on a wonderful sunshine Saturday – the weather conditions had abruptly changed when the professionals started out the next morning. Low level clouds produced cascades of rain, there was a strong wind, and it soon was obvious just how slippery the roads were. One fall followed the other, many with serious consequences. When Raul Alcala somersaulted over a road barrier and found himself on a railway track he had to very happy that the train had just passed a minute before and the next was still some minutes away!

Yet many of the pre-race favourites were still unscathed as the finish got closer even if Lance Armstrong had been involved in two of the crashes. Bjarne Riis, winner of the Tour three years later, attacked bravely with just over two laps to go but the Italian favourites caught him again, and in a counter attack was Miguel Indurain, Tour-winner 1991-95, Frans Maassen and Dag-Otto Lauritzen. The latter, a Norwegian rider who had miraculously survived a parachute accident to come back to the top. In 1987 he won a Tour stage in the Pyrénées arriving alone in Luz Ardiden – a giant surprise – and today he wanted the ultimate triumph in front of his home crowd.

That was not to be. Instead the athletic, intensely motivated Lance Armstrong moved to the front on the last climb. He went over the top among the first but made his move on the descent. He did that often, knowing that the other riders seem to be more off-guard when the descent became steep. Maassen did not think that Armstrong was serious but he was, and much to everybody's surprise he arrived at the finish line with such an advance that he had time to celebrate for several hundred yards, to smile, to laugh, to make finger kisses at the audience, and to present his characteristic triumphant fist gesture.

"No, I did not expect it" he repeatedly told everybody shortly after when he had embraced his team mates and, of course, his mother before going to the podium to receive his gold medal. What a win! Defeating two great riders of the era, Miguel Indurain (2nd) and Olaf Ludwig (3rd) to become the youngest ever rider to win the World Title. And so what a year! Some people asked if there were more ambitions left in his career while others pointed to the fact that if he could improve on his time trailing and be stronger in the mountains, he could be a serious challenger to Miguel Indurain in the Tour.

1994 was a decent year, but no more. Second in the World Cup classics Liège-Bastogne-Liège and Clasica San Sebastian was all right, but victories were what mattered. For the second time he did not win the big American stage race, Tour Dupont, but won a stage, and he came 7th in the World Championship Road race in Italy. In 1995 he won three stages and the overall Tour Dupont, won a stage in Paris-Nice and was motivated for the Tour which was, however, not happy for the Motorola team when Fabio Casartelli died in a terrible crash in the Pyrénées. The young Italian had won that race in Barcelona in 1992 (the Olympic road race) which had been such a disappointment for Armstrong who now realised just how dangerous his occupation was. He finally got his revenge in San Sebastian some three weeks later after a tactical masterpiece which involved a long breakaway with Laurent Jalabert followed by a final escape together with Della Santa again robbing Miguel Indurain of a much sought after victory. Armstrong immediately dedicated this win to Casartelli.

In 1996 Armstrong finally was able to dominate the Tour Dupont completely: Five stage wins and the overall classification. In Europe he added the semi classic Fleche Wallone to his palmarés, came second in the race to the sun, Paris-Nice, and the tough 264km Liège-Bastogne-Liège and finished 7th in the overall World Cup rankings. As 1996 was the last year of the Motorola team, he was offered a contract by the new French team Cofidis and with their backing seemed headed for another career high in 1997. Fate, however, had other plans.

On 2 October 1996 he learned that he was suffering from a testicular cancer which might even be at a point where it had metastasised to other parts of the body. A terrible blow which would have been fatal just a few years earlier when the prognosis for that illness was almost hopeless. This is, however, one cancer towards which medical science has made huge advances, and Armstrong was among those who benefited from that. He fought it desperately, at the same time experiencing the disappointment he felt with the treatment he received from the Cofidis team. Of course they were disappointed not to be able to field their ace but Armstrong had not wanted to be sick and even cyclists should have some rights when they are ill. The American felt that also for that reason he had something to prove when he had recovered.

Even if he was Lance Armstrong 1, he may have had some consolation in the fact that Greg LeMond, too, after being shot during a turkey hunt, had been close to death but succeeded in returning, even winning two more Tours. The second American super champion wanted to do the same. His contract with Cofidis came to an end and he signed a contract with an American team sponsored by the US-Postal Service and prepared his come-back. He had married and bought a villa on the French Riviera where he would spend some of the year. But he still resided in Austin. Everything was ready for the big surprise come-back.

It is easy enough in the fairy tales. You experience bad times and difficult set-backs, but then you get your just reward and are happy and winning ever after. Though reality can be less fair.

After 518 days without racing Armstrong was back for Ruta del Sol 15 February 1998 and finished a respectable 15th. Paris-Nice was next, and... sensation. After a not too successful prologue Armstrong disappeared. Where to? Nobody really knew. He had vanished into thin air and was never expected to be back again. No surprise. His task had been too big and demanding.

A mental breakdown? He had no reason to be disappointed with his come-back. He overreacted. Nobody can overcome a cancer and return directly to the absolute top but in his mind he had thought otherwise. He was disappointed, he panicked, he went back to Texas and spent a month playing golf and drinking beer with old friends. No cycling-talk. May be his career was simply over?

He did not know himself when he decided to spent the next month at the training camp in Boone in North Carolina with two friends. They rode their bicycles, day after day, hour after hour. All month it was raining cats and dogs but having moved to the training camp they did not stay indoors. They raced hard and consulted a physiology department of a nearby university. Gradually the will to compete returned.

Not that Armstrong was missing a lot in his palmarés – he just wanted to compare himself to the best again. Also he did a lot for the Cancer Foundation and could add nothing better to their cause than the proof that you could return to the top of one of the world's toughest sports.

Back to Europe, and now his mind and legs were on friendly terms. He won two minor stage races, Tour de Luxembourg and Rheinland Pfalz Rundfahrt in Germany. A collection of fourth places followed, the most flattering being Vuelta a Espana (the Tour of Spain) and the World Road Race Championship in Valkenburg. Now he had proved what he wanted but ambitions were re-raised. He was able to challenge the best in the biggest stage races. He was more powerful in the mountains, stronger at time-trailing. You could see it on his body. Never had he been stronger or more fit. He realised that he was a possible Tour-winner.

His preparations in 1999 were thorough. Missing out the early season races, he won a prologue victory at Dauphiné Libéré, took the King of the Mountains classification, triumphed at the terribly difficult mountain stage to Plateau de Beille in Route du Sud and in the end his fifth Tour participation was a celebration. He won the prologue, crushing all the specialists such as Alex Zülle and Abraham Olano, in overwhelming style. Jaan Kirsipuu took over the yellow jersey on bonus seconds but after the first big time trial Armstrong was back in it, never to let anybody come near. He even won the first of the mountain stages convincingly, and the US-Postal team was in complete control.

His only worry were rumours circulating in the French press that all was not as it seemed. A consequence of the discussion that modern cycling has two speeds, one for the doped and one for the rest. This harmed Armstrong. He had faced death, was fighting for cancer victims and supporting cancer research. You could not point a finger at him. Against cancer he achieved the ultimate triumph when he won the Tour de France and was hailed as a top sportsman and a symbol on the podium in Paris. Now he continued to do some mountain biking and...

The manager interrupted the long speech: – Young man. For some time I thought: This is something. This is fascinating, but no. This is too good to be true. I simply do not believe it. And even if I did, it is just too much, too rosy. This is not the real world. We will never make the audience accept this manuscript. I am sorry but you have to sell the idea to somebody else.

A moustache, poison and blue glasses

Appendices

The story of the Tour

The first start: The Café Réveil-Matin in Montgeron, south of Paris is where 60 riders started from for the first Tour de France in 1903.

The story of the Tour

1902: Géo Lefèvre, a journalist at the newspaper *L'Auto*, has the idea of a Tour de France. His Editor, Henri Desgrange, accepts.

1903: The first Tour. Entry fee: 10 francs. Six stages, one to three rest days between each. Those who give up can continue the race but only for daily prizes. First prize: 3,000 francs. Total prizes: 20,000 gold francs. Italian born Frenchman Maurice Garin famed for his great spirit wins.

1904: The Tour which was nearly the last. First four are disqualified and suspended four months after the finish for taking a train. Henri Cornet becomes the winner.

1905: The Vosges (Ballon d'Alsace) and the Alps (Côte de Laffrey and Col Bayard) are included. No night racing to avoid 'shady' activities. 78 entries, the winner decided by points from daily placings rather than total time. The race is sabotaged, including nails spread to puncture tyres. The final stage is a kilometre time trial into the Parc des Princes.

1906: The Tour goes abroad for the first time, entering German-occupied Alsace-Lorraine. The first red triangle to mark the last kilometre. Winner René Pothier finishes 48 minutes ahead on the Ballon d'Alsace. He kills himself in January 1907, some say due to a broken heart. Only 14 riders finish the thirteen days and 2,870 miles.

1907: Two carloads of officials and sponsors follow the race.

1908: Lucien Petit-Breton finishes more than 23 hours in front of the runner-up. The first double victory after his win the previous year. He publishes *Why I cycle the roads* about himself, the Tour and his pistol-shooting!

1909: Rain and snow mean only 55 of the 154 starters reach the finish. François Faber is the first foreign winner. Separate classes for sponsored and unsponsored riders. Henri Lavione rides the last 6km with a bike on his back after mechanical trouble.

1910: First big stage in the Pyrénées. First pick-up wagon. *L'Auto* doubles its circulation to 300,000 copies sold during the race. Octave Lapize wins.

1911: Paul Duboc (2nd overall) poisoned by a spectator. Desgrange creates the expression *domestique* for Maurice Brocco and disqualifies him – despite winning a stage by 34 minutes – for riding for opponents and not for himself.

1912: Odile Defraye the first Belgian winner. Octave Lapize, the 1910 winner, retires in protest at the co-operation between the Belgians.

1913: The winner is again judged on the combined time. Eugène Christophe carries his bike 14km down the Tourmalet and repairs his front forks.

1914: Philippe Thys of Belgium wins despite a 30-minute penalty for changing tyres on the last but one stage. The Tour finishes only five days before the outbreak of war.

1915–
1918: The war halts racing. Three giants of the Tour; Faber, Lapize and Petit-Breton do not survive.

1919: Teams discontinued. Prizes reach 50,000 francs. Eugene Christophe 'Le Vieux Gaulois' wears the first yellow jersey and comes third overall. The Pélissier brothers win consecutive stages, quit after a row with Desgrange, then speak of drug-taking. Only 11 riders finish the longest race so far. Belgian Firmin Lambot is sponsored by Kub, a beer company.

1920: Belgians dominate, first five places. Philippe Thys the first to win three times.

1921: Press cars for foreign and regional papers. Another Belgian victory, Leon Scieur.

1922: Christophe breaks – and mends – his forks again, this time on the Galibier. Firmin Lambot of Belgium wins again.

1923: New Tourist category for private entrants. Prizes reach 100,000 francs, including 10,000 for the winner. Bikes can be changed for the first time. *L'Auto* reaches 600,000 copies and, after the final stage on July 23, a million. Henri Pélissier wins for France!

1924: Ottavio Bottechia first to lead from start to finish, the so-called 'a course en tête'. The first Italian winner.

1925: *Le Roi de la Pédale* (King of the Pedal) stars Biscot in the first film based on the Tour. Categories reduced to teams and tourists. The legendary Bottechia wins again.

1926: Record distance of 5,745km, with 17 stages and 13 rest days. The first Japanese rider.

1927: 24 stages for the first time, 10 less than 200km.

1928: Nicolas Frantz of Luxembourg repeats his previous year's victory and leads from start to finish despite riding a woman's bike 100km between Metz and Charleville and losing 28 minutes.

1929: The Tour crosses French borders for second time, going into Switzerland. Three classes – teams and two kinds of tourist, individual and regional teams.

1930: Desgrange switches to national teams after a row with the dominant Alcyon factory who has seven Tours to its credit, including the last three. France, Belgium, Spain, Italy and Germany and 60 tourists in regional teams. All riders on anonymous yellow bikes. Charles Pélissier wins eight stages. The first advertising caravan.

1931: Rest days begin to lessen annually until now there are three. The race is still 5,000km.

1932: Bonuses of 4, 3, 2 and one minute for stage winners. A three-minute win brings a three-minute bonus. Prizes reach 700,000 francs, including 30,000 for the winner.

1933: Trueba of Spain wins the first mountain competition. Winner's bonus cut to two minutes. *L'Auto* sells 834,000.

1934: Bonuses cut to 1:30 but introduced on mountains. First long time-trial, 80km from La Roche-sur-Yon to Nantes. Twenty year old René Vietto rides for first time.

1935: Prizes exceed a million francs. First prize kept secret from tax officials. Romain Maes leads from start to end. Francesco Cepeda dies on the Galibier.

1936: Jacques Goddet takes over as organiser when Henri Desgrange falls ill. He is *L'Auto*'s editor-in-chief and his father Victor was the Tour's financial director.

1937: First prize reaches 200,000 francs but prizes total only 800,000. Roger Lapébie notices his bike has been sabotaged and switches to another on his way to winning after the entire Belgian team including race leader Sylvère Maes withdraws. Charlie Holland, first English rider retires on the penultimate stage.

1938: André Leducq and Antonin Magne finish arm-in-arm on the penultimate stage to mark their retirement. Gino Bartali wins the mountain prize and the race over the Izoard.

1939: No Germans, Italians or Spanish. Regional teams from France, Belgium allowed two teams. *Pour le Maillot Jaune* stars Meg Lemonnier, the organiser's sister-in-law. Vietto second to Sylvère Maes.

1940-

1946: War halts racing. Desgrange falls ill and dies 1940. Four years later, new Government halts publication of all newspapers, including *L'Auto*.

1947: L'Auto becomes *L'Equipe*. The Parc des Princes (this year only) and *Le Parisien Libre* join as co-sponsors. Prizes 4,580,000 francs, including 500,000 for the winner. Belgium and Luxembourg on the route for the first time. Jean Robic wins on the last stage without wearing yellow.

1948: Prizes now 7m francs, including 600,000 for the winner, plus a daily bonus for the *maillot jaune*. Two mountain categories. Bartali wins seven stages and triumphs again – his previous victory was 1938.

1949: The Tour goes to Spain for the first time. Three mountain categories. Arch rivals Coppi and Bartali ride for Italy, as Coppi wins at first attempt from Bartali.

1950: Yellow jersey gets 100,00 francs a day. Prizes reach 14m francs thanks to inflation. Orson Welles is the race starter. Two Italian teams pull out after a row with the organisers and San Remo is scrapped as a stage town in favour of Menton, its only time as a finish. Ferdinand Kubler, first Swiss winner.

1951: Mont Ventoux included for the first time. Singer Jacques Grello names Swiss winner Hugo Koblet 'the pedaller of charm.' Zaaf was 'Lanterne Rouge'.

1952: Glorious victory for Coppi by over 28 mins. Alpe d'Huez, Serestrière and the Puy-de-Dôme make their debuts. 100,000 francs a stage for the most aggressive rider. First Tour on TV.

1953: Fifteen winners including Christophe at Parc des Princes for 50th anniversary. Robic picks up a weight of lead to help him down the Tourmalet. First green points jersey. Bobet wins first Tour.

1954: The Tour starts in Amsterdam, its first visit outside France after the war. Federico Bahamontes debuts and wins the mountain competition.

1955: First British team in Tour. Brian Robinson 29th. Charly Gaul of Luxembourg wins in the mountains. Bobet's third consecutive victory.

1956: Roger Walkowiak the first French regional winner. He sets a record average speed of 36.268kmh. Brian Robinson improves on 1955 and comes 14th.

1957: First win by former Hour record holder, Jacques Anquetil.

1958: The Tour starts in Brussels. Gaul's only win. Darrigade collides with an official 50m from the finish, goes to hospital but keeps his prizes. Brian Robinson, riding for an International team, becomes the first Briton to win a stage.

1959: Another stage for Robinson, a solo breakaway at Chalon-sur-Saône. Finishes 19th. Bahamontes wins his only Tour, Spain's first. Prizes 40m with two million for the winner in the last year of 'old' francs.

1960: Four riders take 14:40 lead and one, Gastone Nencini, wins. Roger Rivière breaks his spine in the mountains. Race stops at Colombey-les-deux-Eglises to greet Charles De Gaulle but Beuffeuil rides by after a puncture and wins the stage. Tom Simpson rides in only the second British team (8 riders) to compete in the Tour.

1961: Darrigade wins the first stage for the fifth successive year. Anquetil wins the next and stays in yellow until the end.

1962: Trade teams return. Tommy Simpson finishes 6th, the first Englishman to wear the 'maillot jaune'. Celebrated French film director Louis Malle, makes *Vive le Tour*, a classic film.

1963: Ireland's Seamus Elliott wins at Roubaix to take first stage victory and the first Irishman to wear the yellow jersey. Rik van Looy wins four stages and the green points jersey. Poulidor booed and Anquetil cheered at the Parc des Princes and makes history by winning his fourth Tour de France. English rider Alan Ramsbottom 16th out of 76 finishers.

1964: Anquetil's fourth consecutive Tour and fifth win. Spanish climber, the 'Eagle of Toledo' Federico Bahamontes' sixth mountains win. Future Spanish hero, Miguel Indurain is born.

1965: The Tour starts in Cologne. Felice Gimondi wins, Poulidor second, Claude Lelouche makes his own testimony to the Tour with the acclaimed film, *Pour un Maillot Jaune*.

1966: Riders strike after drug checks start at Bordeaux.

1967: Tommy Simpson dies on Mont Ventoux. The last finish into the Parc des Princes.

1968: Drugs tests on every stage for the first time. First white jersey for the best combined results of all categories. Jan Janssen first Dutchman to win, taking yellow on last stage.

1969: Eddy Merckx rides his first Tour. Wins all three jerseys and a stage from the Tourmalet by eight minutes. No rest day.

1970: Eddy Merckx wins eight stages and overall. Joop Zoetemelk second on first of 16 Tours.

1971: Luis Ocana seriously injured in yellow jersey. Eddy Merckx declines it for a day. First stage is a team time-trial. Rest days reintroduced. First air transfer between stages (Marseille-Albi).

1972: Cyrille Guimard challenges Merckx throughout.

1973: The Tour starts in Leiden, Holland. Ocana dominates in Merckx's absence.

1974: First stage in Britain (Plympton). Joël Santori makes *La Course en Tête* about Merckx, who wins eight stages.

1975: First finish on the Champs-Elysées. First polkadot jersey. White jersey now for best young rider. Merckx hit by spectator on Puy-de-Dôme; receives Légion d'Honneur before the start in Charleroi.

1976: Prizes pass a million new francs. Winner Lucien van Impe gets a flat (100,000 francs). Merckx wins eight stages.

1977: Didi Thurau wears yellow for two weeks in his debut. Bernard Thévenet's only victory.

1978: Bernard Hinault wins debut Tour. Yellow jersey Michel Pollentier caught defrauding dope check. Walking strike at Valence d'Agen.

1979: Hinault wins after battle with Zoetemelk. Agostinho third at 37.

1980: Phil Anderson the first Australian yellow jersey. The film *23 days in July* made about him.

1982: The Tour starts in Berne. Just 3,507km and 21 stages long. Hinault wins the Tour, Giro and Grand Prix des Nations.

1983: Colombian amateurs ride, followed by 32 Colombian journalists. Laurent Fignon wins at first attempt.

1984: Red jersey for daily sprint competition. Luis Herrera first South American stage winner (Alpe d'Huez). Dustin Hoffman follows several stages for uncompleted film, *The Yellow Jersey*.

1985: Hinault third to win Tour five times, despite a bad crash. First solid wheels.

1986: Prize-fund increases from 3 to 4.5m francs in three years. Greg LeMond first American winner.

1987: Hinault becomes race technical director. Prizes now 6.3m francs. Record 209 riders start from Berlin. Stephen Roche is the first Irish winner. His victories in the Giro and World Championships in a glory year saw him equal the feat of Eddy Merckx in 1974.

1988: Spanish star Pedro Delgado wins despite dope scandal. Prizes now 7.5m francs, including a car worth 1.3m as part of first prize.

1989: Greg LeMond – with tribars – wins by a margin of eight seconds after beating Laurent Fignon in the closing time-trial. Eighteen of 22 teams chosen from world rankings for first time. Pedro Delgado loses three minutes after starting the prologue late.

1990: Greg LeMond's third victory. 2m francs for the winner, 8m for the rest. Jerseys cut to yellow, green and polkadot. 3,500 journalists represent 348 publications and broadcasters.

1991: Miguel Indurain's first win.

1992: Start in San Sebastian, Spain. Many foreign visits. Miguel Indurain adds Tour to his Giro.

1993: Miguel Indurain takes Tour and Giro.

1994: Britain hosts two stages; Brighton and Portsmouth. Chris Boardman wears the 'maillot jaune'.

1995: Indurain first to win five successive Tours. Bjarne Riis first Dane in top three. Fabio Casartelli dies in crash.

1996: Indurain is dethroned by Bjarne Riis, the first Danish winner. Germany's Telekom team dominates; Jan Ullrich is second, Erik Zabel wins the green jersey and Telekom takes the team competition.

1997: Jan Ullrich wins; Richard Virenque first to win mountains competition in four successive years.

1998: Huge doping scandal sees half the field disqualified or abandoned. The Italian climbing star, Marco Pantani wins.

1999: Lance Armstrong becomes the second American to win the Tour. Following his recovery from cancer this is one of the greatest come-backs in sporting history.

Tour de France Winners

Calm demeanor: Five-times overall winner of the Tour de France, Miguel Indurain shares this illustrious record with Jacques Anquetil, Eddy Merckx and Bernard Hinault.

Tour de France Winners

Yellow Jersey Winners

Year	Winner	Time	Distance	Stages	Starters	Finishers	Av. Speed
1903	Maurice Garin (FRA)	94h33'00"	2,428	6	60	21	25,679
1904	Henri Cornet (FRA)	96h05'56"	2,428	6	88	27	25,265
1905	Louis Trousselier (FRA)	110h26'56"	2,994	11	60	24	27,107
1906	René Pottier (FRA)	189h34'00"	4,637	13	82	14	24,463
1907	Lucien Petit-Breton (FRA)	158h45'05"	4,488	14	93	33	28,470
1908	Lucien Petit-Breton (FRA)	156h53'29"	4,488	14	112	36	28,740
1909	François Faber (LUX)	157h01'22"	4,497	14	150	55	28,658
1910	Octave Lapize (FRA)	162h41'30"	4,734	15	110	41	29,099
1911	Gustave Garrigou (FRA)	195h37'00"	5,343	15	84	28	27,322
1912	Odile Defraye (BEL)	190h30'28"	5,289	15	131	41	27,763
1913	Philippe Thys (BEL)	197h54'00"	5,287	15	140	25	26,715
1914	Philippe Thys (BEL)	200h28'48"	5,380	15	145	54	26,835
1919	Firmin Lambot (BEL)	231h07'15"	5,560	15	69	11	24,056
1920	Philippe Thys (BEL)	228h36'13"	5,503	15	113	22	24,072
1921	Léon Scieur (BEL)	221h50'26"	5,485	15	123	38	24,724
1922	Firmin Lambot (BEL)	222h08'06"	5,375	15	121	38	24,196
1923	Henri Pélissier (FRA)	222h15'30"	5,386	15	139	48	24,233
1924	Ottavio Bottecchia (ITA)	226h18'21"	5,425	15	157	60	24,250
1925	Ottavio Bottecchia (ITA)	219h10'18"	5,440	18	130	49	24,820
1926	Lucien Buysse (BEL)	238h44'25"	5,745	17	126	41	24,273
1927	Nicolas Frantz (LUX)	198h16'42"	5,398	24	142	39	27,224
1928	Nicolas Frantz (LUX)	192h48'58"	5,476	22	162	41	28,400
1929	Maurice Dewaele (BEL)	186h39'16"	5,286	22	155	60	28,319
1930	André Leducq (FRA)	172h12'16"	4,822	21	100	59	28,000
1931	Antonin Magne (FRA)	177h10'03"	5,091	24	81	35	28,735
1932	André Leducq (FRA)	154h12'59"	4,479	21	80	57	29,047
1933	Georges Speicher (FRA)	147h51'37"	4,395	23	80	40	29,818
1934	Antonin Magne (FRA)	147h13'58"	4,470	23	60	39	30,360
1935	Romain Maes (BEL)	141h23'00"	4,338	21	93	46	30,650
1936	Sylvere Maes (FRA)	142h47'32"	4,442	21	90	43	31,108
1937	Roger Lapébie (FRA)	138h58'31"	4,415	20	98	46	31,768
1938	Gino Bartali (ITA)	148h29'12"	4,694	21	96	55	31,565
1939	Sylvere Maes (BEL)	132h03'17"	4,224	18	79	49	31,986
1947	Jean Robic (FRA)	148h11'25"	4,640	21	99	53	31,412
1948	Gino Bartali (ITA)	147h10'36"	4,922	21	120	44	33,442
1949	Fausto Coppi (ITA)	149h40'49"	4,808	21	120	55	32,121
1950	Ferdi Kubler (SUI)	145h36'56"	4,773	22	116	51	32,778
1951	Hugo Koblet (SUI)	142h20'14"	4,690	24	123	66	32,949
1952	Fausto Coppi (ITA)	151h57'20"	4,898	23	122	78	32,233
1953	Louison Bobet (FRA)	129h23'25"	4,476	22	119	76	34,593
1954	Louison Bobet (FRA)	140h06'05"	4,656	23	110	69	33,229
1955	Louison Bobet (FRA)	130h29'26"	4,495	22	130	69	34,446
1956	Roger Walkowiak (FRA)	124h01'16"	4,498	22	120	88	36,268
1957	Jacques Anquetil (FRA)	135h44'42"	4,686	22	120	56	34,520
1958	Charly Gaul (LUX)	116h59'05"	4,319	24	120	78	36,919
1959	Federico Bahamontes (ESP)	123h46'45"	4,391	22	120	65	35,474
1960	Gastone Nencini (ITA)	112h08'42"	4,173	22	128	81	37,210
1961	Jacques Anquetil (FRA)	122h01'33"	4,397	21	132	72	36,033

Year	Winner	Time	Distance	Stages	Starters	Finishers	Av. Speed
1962	Jacques Anquetil (FRA)	114h31'45"	4,274	22	150	94	37,317
1963	Jacques Anquetil (FRA)	113h30'05"	4,210	21	130	76	37,092
1964	Jacques Anquetil (FRA)	127h09'44"	4,504	22	132	81	35,419
1965	Felice Gimondi (ITA)	116h42'06"	4,188	22	130	96	35,886
1966	Lucien Aimar (FRA)	117h34'21"	4,329	22	130	82	36,760
1967	Roger Pingeon (FRA)	136h53'50"	4,780	22	130	88	34,756
1968	Jan Janssen (NED)	133h49'32"	4,492	22	110	63	33,556
1969	Eddy Merckx (BEL)	116h16'02"	4,117	22	130	86	35,409
1970	Eddy Merckx (BEL)	119h31'49"	4,254	23	150	100	35,589
1971	Eddy Merckx (BEL)	96h45'14"	3,608	25	130	94	38,084
1972	Eddy Merckx (BEL)	108h17'18"	3,846	20	132	88	35,514
1973	Luis Ocana (ESP)	122h25'34"	4,090	20	132	87	33,407
1974	Eddy Merckx (BEL)	116h16'58"	4,098	22	130	105	35,241
1975	Bernard Thévenet (FRA)	114h35'31"	4,000	22	140	86	34,906
1976	Lucien Van Impe (BEL)	116h22'23"	4,017	22	130	87	34,518
1977	Bernard Thévenet (FRA)	115h38'30"	4,096	22	100	53	35,419
1978	Bernard Hinault (FRA)	108h18'00"	3,908	22	110	78	36,084
1979	Bernard Hinault (FRA)	103h06'50"	3,765	24	150	90	36,513
1980	Joop Zoetemelk (NED)	109h19'14"	3,842	22	130	85	35,144
1981	Bernard Hinault (FRA)	96h19'38"	3,753	24	150	121	38,960
1982	Bernard Hinault (FRA)	92h08'46"	3,507	21	169	125	38,059
1983	Laurent Fignon (FRA)	105h07'52"	3,809	22	140	88	36,230
1984	Laurent Fignon (FRA)	112h03'40"	4,021	23	170	124	35,882
1985	Bernard Hinault (FRA)	113h24'23"	4,109	22	180	144	36,232
1986	Greg LeMond (USA)	110h35'19"	4,094	23	210	132	37,020
1987	Stephen Roche (IRL)	115h27'42"	4,231	25	207	135	36,645
1988	Pedro Delgado (ESP)	84h27'53"	3,286	22	198	151	38,909
1989	Greg LeMond (USA)	87h38'35"	3,285	21	198	138	37,487
1990	Greg LeMond (USA)	90h43'20"	3,504	21	198	156	38,621
1991	Miguel Indurain (ESP)	101h01'20"	3,914	22	198	158	38,747
1992	Miguel Indurain (ESP)	100h49'30"	3,983	21	198	130	39,504
1993	Miguel Indurain (ESP)	95h57'09"	3,714	20	180	136	38,709
1994	Miguel Indurain (ESP)	103h38'38"	3,978	21	189	117	38,383
1995	Miguel Indurain (ESP)	92h44'59"	3,635	20	189	115	39,193
1996	Bjarne Riis (DEN)	95h57'16"	3,765	21	189	129	39,227
1997	Jan Ullrich (GER)	100h30'35"	3,943	21	198	139	39,230
1998	Marco Pantani (ITA)	92h59'46"	3,711	21	189	96	39,983
1999	Lance Armstrong (USA)	91h32'16"	3,690	20	180	141	40.273

Green Jersey Winners

Year	Winner	Year	Winner
1953	Fritz Schaer (SUI)	1977	Jaques Esclassan (FRA)
1954	Ferdi Kubler (SUI)	1978	Freddy Maertens (BEL)
1955	Stan Ockers (BEL)	1979	Bernard Hinault (FRA)
1956	Stan Ockers (BEL)	1980	Rudy Pevenage (BEL)
1957	Jean Forestier (FRA)	1981	Freddy Maertens (BEL)
1958	Jean Graczyk (FRA)	1982	Sean Kelly (IRL)
1959	André Darrigade (FRA)	1983	Sean Kelly (IRL)
1960	Jean Graczyk (FRA)	1984	Frank Hoste (BEL)
1961	André Darrigade (FRA)	1985	Sean Kelly (IRL)
1962	Rudi Altig (GER)	1986	Eric Vanderaerden (BEL)
1963	Rik Van Looy (BEL)	1987	Jean Paul Van Poppel (NED)
1964	Jan Janssen (NED)	1988	Eddy Planckaert (BEL)
1965	Jan Janssen (NED)	1989	Sean Kelly (IRL)
1966	Willy Plankaert (BEL)	1990	Olaf Ludwig (GER)
1967	Jan Janssen (NED)	1991	Djamoldine Abdoujaparov (UZB)
1968	Franco Bitossi (ITA)	1992	Laurent Jalabert (FRA)
1969	Eddy Merckx (BEL)	1993	Djamolodine Abdujaparov (UZB)
1970	Walter Godefroot (BEL)	1994	Djamolodine Abdujaparov (UZB)
1971	Eddy Merckx (BEL)	1995	Laurent Jalabert (FRA)
1972	Eddy Merckx (BEL)	1996	Erik Zabel (GER)
1973	Herman Van Springel (BEL)	1997	Erik Zabel (GER)
1974	Patrick Sercu (BEL)	1998	Erik Zabel (GER)
1975	Rik Van Linden (BEL)	1999	Erik Zabel (GER)
1976	Freddy Maertens (BEL)		

Almost unstoppable: Apart from five overall Tour wins, Eddy Merckx won the Green Jersey on three occasions.

King of the Mounatins Winners

Year	Winner
1933	Vincente Trueba (ESP)
1934	René Vietto (FRA)
1935	Félicien Vervaecke (BEL)
1936	Julian Berrendero (ESP)
1937	Félicien Vervaecke (BEL)
1938	Gino Bartali (ITA)
1939	Sylvere Maes (BEL)
1947	Pierre Brambilla (ITA)
1948	Gino Bartali (ITA)
1949	Fausto Coppi (ITA)
1950	Louison Bobet (FRA)
1951	Raphaël Géminiani (FRA)
1952	Fausto Coppi (ITA)
1953	Jesus Lorono (ESP)
1954	Federico Bahamontes (ESP)
1955	Charly Gaul (LUX)
1956	Charly Gaul (LUX)
1957	Gastone Nencini (ITA)
1958	Federico Bahamontes (ESP)
1959	Federico Bahamontes (ESP)
1960	Imerio Massignan (ITA)
1961	Imerio Massignan (ITA)
1962	Federico Bahamontes (ESP)
1963	Federico Bahamontes (ESP)
1964	Federico Bahamontes (ESP)
1965	Julio Jimenez (ESP)
1966	Julio Jimenez (ESP)
1967	Julio Jimenez (ESP)
1968	Aurelio Gonzalez (ESP)
1969	Eddy Merckx (BEL)
1970	Eddy Merckx (BEL)
1971	Lucien Van Impe (BEL)
1972	Lucien Van Impe (BEL)
1973	Pedro Torres (ESP)
1974	Domingo Perurena (ESP)
1975	Lucien Van Impe (BEL)
1976	Giancarlo Bellini (ITA)
1977	Lucien Van Impe (BEL)
1978	Mariano Martinez (FRA)
1979	Giovanni Battaglin (ITA)
1980	Raymond Martin (FRA)
1981	Lucien Van Impe (BEL)
1982	Bernard Vallet (FRA)
1983	Lucien Van Impe (BEL)
1984	Robert Millar (GB)
1985	Luis Herrera (COL)
1986	Bernard Hinault (FRA)
1987	Luis Herrera (COL)

Year	Winner
1988	Steven Rooks (NED)
1989	Gert-Jan Theunisse (NED)
1990	Thierry Claveyrolat (FRA)
1991	Claudio Chiappucci (ITA)
1992	Claudio Chiappucci (ITA)
1993	Tony Rominger (SUI)
1994	Richard Virenque (FRA)
1995	Richard Virenque (FRA)
1996	Richard Virenque (FRA)
1997	Richard Virenque (FRA)
1998	Christophe Rinero (FRA)
1999	Richard Virenque (FRA)

Climbers supreme:
Between 1954 and 1964, Charly Gaul (left)
and Federico Bahamontes won the King of
the Mountains competition eight times.

Team Classification Winners

Year	Winner	Year	Winner
1930	France	1969	Faema
1931	Belgium	1970	Salvarani
1932	Italy	1971	Bic
1933	France	1972	GAN-Mercier
1934	France	1973	Bic
1935	Belgium	1974	Kas
1936	Belgium	1975	GAN-Mercier
1937	France	1976	Kas
1938	Belgium	1977	TI-Raleigh
1939	Belgium	1978	Miko-Mercier
1947	Italy	1979	Renault-Gitane
1948	Belgium	1980	Miko-Mercier
1949	Italy	1981	Peugeot-Esso
1950	Belgium	1982	Coop-Mercier
1951	France	1983	TI-Raleigh
1952	Italy	1984	Renault-Elf
1953	Netherlands	1985	La Vie Claire
1954	Switzerland	1986	La Vie Claire
1955	France	1987	Système U
1956	Belgium	1988	PDM
1957	France	1989	PDM
1958	Belgium	1990	Z
1959	Belgium	1991	Banesto
1960	France	1992	Carrera
1961	France	1993	Carrera
1962	St. Raphaël-H.	1994	Festina-Andorra
1963	St. Raphaël-G.	1995	ONCE
1964	Pelforth-S.	1996	Festina
1965	Kas	1997	Telekom
1966	Kas	1998	Cofidis
1967	France	1999	Banesto
1968	Spain		

Index